UNIT30

Rhayader lives alone on the Great Marsh. One day a child approaches his home with an injured bird.

This story is taken from a book called *The Snow Goose* by Paul Gallico.

The Lost Princess

One November afternoon, three years after Rhayader had come to the Great Marsh, a child approached the lighthouse studio by means of the sea wall. In her arms she carried a burden.

She was no more than twelve, slender, dirty, nervous and timid as a bird, but beneath the grime as eerily beautiful as a marsh faery. She was pure Saxon, large-boned, fair, with a head to which her body was yet to grow, and deep-set, violet-coloured eyes.

She was desperately frightened of the ugly man she had come to see, for legend had already begun to gather about Rhayader, and the native wild-fowlers hated him for interfering with their sport.

But greater than her fear was the need of that which she bore. For locked in her child's heart was the knowledge, picked up somewhere in the swampland, that this ogre who lived in the lighthouse had magic that could heal injured things.

She had never seen Rhayader before and was close to fleeing in panic at the dark apparition that appeared at the studio door, drawn by her footsteps—the black head and beard, the sinister hump, and the crooked claw.

She stood there staring, poised like a disturbed marsh bird for instant flight.

But his voice was deep and kind when he spoke to her.

'What is it, child?'

She stood her ground, and then edged timidly forward. The thing she carried in her arms was a large white bird, and it was quite still. There were stains of blood on its whiteness and on her kirtle where she had held it to her.

The girl placed it in his arms. 'I found it, sir. It's hurted. Is it still alive?'

2

'Yes. Yes, I think so. Come in, child, come in.'

Rhayader went inside, bearing the bird, which he placed upon a table, where it moved feebly. Curiosity overcame fear. The girl followed and found herself in a room warmed by a coal fire, shining with many coloured pictures that covered the walls, and full of a strange but pleasant smell.

The bird fluttered. With his good hand Rhayader spread one of its immense white pinions. The end was beautifully tipped with black.

Rhayader looked and marvelled, and said: 'Child! where did you find it?'

'In t' marsh, sir, where fowlers had been. What—what is it, sir?'

'It's a snow goose from Canada. But how in all heaven came it here?'

The name seemed to mean nothing to the little girl. Her deep violet eyes, shining out of the dirt on her thin face, were fixed with concern on the injured bird.

She said: 'Can 'ee heal it, sir?'

'Yes, yes,' said Rhayader. 'We will try. Come, you shall help me.'

There were scissors and bandages and splints on a shelf, and he was marvellously deft, even with the crooked claw that managed to hold things.

He said: 'Ah, she has been shot, poor thing. Her leg is broken, and the wing tip, but not badly. See, we will clip her primaries, so that we can bandage it, but in the spring the feathers will grow and she will be able to fly again. We'll bandage it close to her body, so that she cannot move it until it has set, and then make a splint for the poor leg.'

Her fears forgotten, the child watched, fascinated, as he worked, and all the more so because while he fixed a fine splint to the shattered leg he told her the most wonderful story.

The bird was a young one, no more than a year old. She was born in a northern land far, far across the seas, a land belonging to England. Flying to the south to escape the snow and ice and bitter cold, a great storm had seized her and whirled and buffeted her about. It was a truly terrible storm, stronger than her great wings, stronger than anything. For days and nights it held her in its grip and there was nothing she could do but fly before it. When finally it had blown itself out and her sure instincts took her south again, she was over a different land and surrounded by strange birds that she had never seen before. At last, exhausted by her ordeal, she had sunk to rest in a friendly green marsh, only to be met by the blast from the hunter's gun.

'A bitter reception for a visiting princess,' concluded Rhayader. 'We will call her "*La Princesse Perdue*," the Lost Princess. And in a few days she will be feeling much better. See!' He reached into his pocket and produced a handful of grain. The snow goose opened its round yellow eyes and nibbled at it.

The child laughed with delight, and then suddenly caught her breath with alarm as the full import of where she was pressed in upon her, and without a word she turned and fled out of the door.

'Wait, wait!' cried Rhayader, and went to the entrance, where he stopped so that it framed his dark bulk. The girl was already fleeing down the sea wall, but she paused at his voice and looked back.

'What is your name, child?'

'Frith.'

'Eh?' said Rhayader. 'Fritha, I suppose. Where do you live?'

'Wi' t' fisherfolk at Wickaeldroth.' She gave the name the old Saxon pronunciation.

'Will you come back tomorrow, or the next day, to see how the Princess is getting along?'

She paused, and again Rhayader must have thought of the wild water birds caught motionless in that split second of alarm before they took to flight.

But her thin voice came back to him: 'Ay!'

And then she was gone, with her fair hair streaming out behind her.

The snow goose mended rapidly and by mid-winter was already limping about the enclosure with the wild pink-footed geese with which it associated, rather than the barnacles, and had learned to come to be fed at Rhayader's call. And the child, Fritha, or Frith, was a frequent visitor. She had overcome her fear of Rhayader. Her imagination was captured by the presence of this strange white princess from a land far over the sea, a land that was all pink, as she knew from the map that Rhayader showed her, and on which they traced the stormy path of the lost bird from its home in Canada to the Great Marsh of Essex.

Then one June morning a group of late pink-feet, fat and well fed from the winter at the lighthouse, answered the stronger call of the breeding-grounds and rose lazily, climbing into the sky in ever widening circles. With them, her white body and black-tipped pinions shining in the spring sun, was the snow goose. It so happened that Frith was at the lighthouse. Her cry brought Rhayader running from the studio.

'Look! Look! The Princess! Be she going away?'

Rhayader stared into the sky at the climbing specks. 'Ay,' he said, unconsciously dropping into her manner of speech. 'The Princess is going home. Listen! she is bidding us farewell.'

Out of the clear sky came the mournful barking of the pink-feet, and above it the higher, clearer note of the snow goose. The specks drifted northward, formed into a tiny V, diminished, and vanished.

With the departure of the snow goose ended the visits of Frith to the lighthouse. Rhayader learned all over again the meaning of the word 'loneliness.'

That summer, out of his memory, he painted a picture of a slender, grime-covered child, her fair hair blown by a November storm, who bore in her arms a wounded white bird.

To think and talk about

A 1. Why does Rhayader live in the marsh alone?

   2. Why do you think Rhayader was so keen to know Frith's name and whether she would come back to see the bird or not?

   3. How much of Rhayader's story of the snow goose do you think was true?

   4. Why did Rhayader paint a picture of Frith and the snow goose after they had both gone?

B 1. Do you think the snow goose will ever return? Give some reasons for your answer.

   2. Why do you think Frith stops visiting Rhayader when the snow goose leaves?

   3. What legends do you imagine had grown up about Rhayader?

   4. How do you imagine Rhayader and Frith felt when they saw the snow goose join the pink-footed geese in flight?

C 1. If you were Frith or Rhayader what would you have done when the snow goose left?

   2. Would you have tried to prevent the bird from leaving or do you think it should be free to go?

   3. How do you feel about Rhayader?

   4. In what ways are Frith and Rhayader similar to each other?

More books to read

1. *The House of Wings* by Betsy Byars
   Sammy didn't take to his grandfather at once. In fact, he ran off and the old man had to follow. Then they came across an injured bird—a huge crane—and things began to change.

2. *The Wheel on the School* by Meindert De Jong
   A happy story of how children persuade storks to come back and nest in their village.

3. *The Dolphin Crossing* by Jill Paton Walsh
   The British army was stranded on the beach at Dunkirk. This is the story of two boys who took a boat to help save the soldiers.

Something Told the Wild Geese

Something told the wild geese
  It was time to go.
Though the fields lay golden
  Something whispered—'Snow'.
Leaves were green and stirring,
  Berries, lustre-glossed,
But beneath warm feathers
  Something cautioned—'Frost'.

All the sagging orchards
  Steamed with amber spice,
But each wild beast stiffened
  At remembered ice.
Something told the wild geese
  It was time to fly—
Summer sun was on their wings,
  Winter in their cry.

Rachel Field

To write about

Imagine you are Rhayader.
Could you write the story of the day the snow goose returns?

Searching for missing words

In the passage some words have been missed out.
Can you be sure which words have been missed out?
Sometimes there can be only one answer.
Sometimes there can be several answers for you to think and
talk about.
How many words can you find?

They walked on, through a maze of streets, and nothing
happened except that Miss Fisher's shopping bag grew
bulkier and bulkier. Then the street they were in took a _____
turn and opened out into the _____ road round the Park. Miss
Fisher _____ smartly across the pedestrian crossing. Uncle
Joseph _____ her, but by the time Ben _____ the kerb, the
traffic had begun to _____. Ben fretted on the pavement.

By _____ time he was able to _____, Uncle Joseph had
vanished. But he _____ still see Miss Fisher, straight-backed
and _____, walking into the Park over the _____ canal. She
seemed sure, as she _____ been sure when she was
shopping, _____ where she wanted to go. Though the _____
were winding and pleasant, she marched _____ with military
briskness like a _____ on parade.

From *On the Run* by Nina Bawden

Is it in the passage?

Karla wrote this letter about **books** for her school magazine.

Dear Editor,
Children all love a good ghost story. Everybody knows this is a fact, so why are there so few good ones around? I think I've read a fair number, but I can only think of three or four that really scared me. Now if a ghost story doesn't really scare you then it's not much use! Too many stories try the same old ghost lines. We have to read about rattling chains and headless horsemen and that sort of thing. These stories frighten no-one. A ghost story that will is called 'Strange Times at the Manor House'. I won't spoil the story for you but be careful. It will make your hair stand on end. That is if it doesn't turn pure white! You've been warned!

Yours faithfully,
Karla

Read the sentences below and then put them into three groups:
   (a) Facts which are in the passage
   (b) Opinions which are in the passage
   (c) Facts or opinions which are *not* in the passage.

1. It is a well known fact that all children love a good ghost story.
2. Karla has read three or four stories that frightened her.
3. There are not many good ghost stories around.
4. Stories about headless horsemen are the most frightening.
5. Karla has read 'Strange Times at the Manor House'.
6. The story 'Strange Times at the Manor House' is spoiled by Karla.
7. If a ghost story doesn't frighten you it is not much good.
8. When Karla saw a ghost her hair stood on end.
9. Karla likes ghost stories.
10. 'Strange Times at the Manor House' will really frighten you.

What's the truth?

Here is a picture of Mr Forbes the horse dealer buying a pony from Mr and Mrs Collins.

What else do you think Mr Forbes will say about the pony?

Here is Mr Forbes a few days later selling the pony to Mr and Mrs White.

What else do you think he will *now* be saying about the pony? Talk about how words can be used to give a good or a bad impression.

Here is a group of sentences which make a story.
They are in the wrong order.
Can you put the story in the correct order?

(a) Each year he planned to return but something turned up to prevent him.

(b) Despite the fact that he was exhausted from travelling thousands of miles he felt great joy as the bus entered his village.

(c) In fact, he wondered if his heart had ever really left the beautiful village.

(d) Now with old age approaching, he had been determined to make the journey.

(e) The village where Mario was born was high in the Italian hills.

(f) It hadn't changed much and as he walked about the familiar streets, the years slipped away and he was a boy again.

(g) Twenty years previously he had left to find employment abroad.

Read and remember

Can you read carefully and remember what you've read?
Here is a short story. Read it carefully and try to remember the
events as they are told in the story.
Do you think you'll remember when you turn to page 18?

The Street at Night

The children leave their games when the last light of the day
disappears. Mothers and fathers shout to their children to come
for supper. Slowly they obey and leave the street.

Silence for a while. The occasional car rumbles past and the
bus taking the night workers to the factory. The street lamps
glow and gradually brighten, casting their pools of light here and
there. Doors open in two or three places and cats emerge to sniff
the air before moving off on secret missions.

Blinds are drawn, bedroom lights go on, and from the chip
shop, a strong distinctive smell floats up the street. Dogs return
home whining to be fed and scratch at their doors until they are
let in. Just as everything seems to settle, the cries of a child
unwilling to go to bed are clearly heard. It doesn't last for long
and a bedroom light going out signals mother's victory.

Again silence descends. Smoke curls up from the chimney
tops. One by one the lights go out until only a few late night
viewers are left. The street is at peace, resting in preparation for
the adventures of tomorrow.

Now turn to page 18.

To talk and write about

1. Don't go by appearances!
   Rhayader frightened Frith because to her he looked like an
   'ogre' yet he turned out to be a kind man.
   Imagine you meet someone who appears to be mean and
   turns out to be very generous.
   Can you write a story about this meeting?
2. Have you ever been lost?
   Write about how you felt and how you managed to find your
   way home.
3. Can you write a careful description of a bird or animal you
   know well?

Beginnings

The answer to each of the five clues starts with the same letters.
Each answer is a word. The beginning letters are given in
capitals.
Use you dictionary to find the answers.

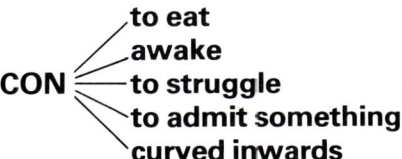

CON
- to eat
- awake
- to struggle
- to admit something
- curved inwards

Reading for the main idea

Katrina was working on a project about **Switzerland** and came across this passage in a book.

Although one of the smallest countries in Europe, Switzerland is one of the most beautiful, with a wide variety of scenery. To get to neighbouring countries by land you have to use railway tunnels and passes high in the mountains or alps. In winter these often become blocked by snow and avalanches. Great glaciers are formed here and the water which flows from beneath them becomes the start of many rivers. Hydro-electric power is often made from waterfalls formed in the mountains. As the winter snow melts, cattle can graze in the high alpine pastures, which are very rich, and many dairy products are made. Grass grown on these slopes is used for fodder in winter when the cattle return to lower ground. This country with its high peaks is famous for its skiing, tobogganing, skating, and mountain climbing.

Katrina made notes of the main ideas of this passage. Here is part of the diagram she made. Can you add the other main ideas and use arrows to show supporting details?

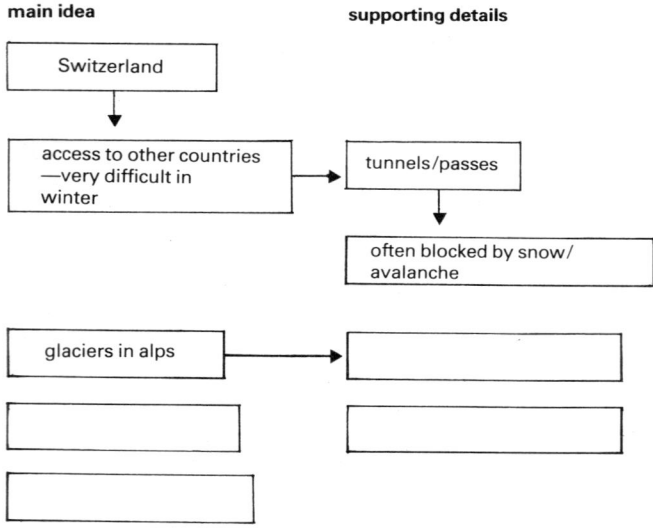

16

Act it out

Do you think Frith's parents were pleased when they found out that she had visited Rhayader?

Talk about what they might have said to her when they found out.

Act a scene in which they ask her about her visits to the man. What will she say?

How will the scene end?

Read and remember

Can you put the sentences below in the same order as in the story 'The Street at Night' on page 14?
Don't look back to the story.

(a) For a while there is silence except for a few cars moving and some cats coming out for the night.

(b) Once more silence reigns and slowly the lights go out as people go to sleep to prepare for the next day.

(c) Children leave their games as the light fades and they slowly obey the call of parents to come for supper.

(d) Bedroom lights go on and blinds are drawn, dogs return home, and the smell from the chip shop floats up the street.

(e) As peace settles the cry of a child is heard but that doesn't last long.

The company words keep

Sid was writing a story about being in a haunted house.
His teacher thought there were parts of the story which could have been written in a more interesting way.
One sentence Sid wrote was this:

The house was very spooky.

Here are some of Sid's classmates' suggestions for improving the sentence:

The house felt as though it might be haunted.
The house felt sad, but frightening at the same time.
The house had a strange air.

Can you make any more suggestions?
Which way do you think is best? Why?
Do they all have roughly the same sense as Sid's sentence?

Below is a paragraph from Sid's story. There are parts which could be improved. Try to decide which they are, and talk about ways of improving them.

> The house was very spooky. I heard a noise behind me and got a fright. It was funny but I suddenly felt cold. I could just see something there in the dark. I was very frightened and ran till I got home.

Find a story which you have written recently. Are there parts of it which could be written in a more interesting way?

Here is a poem called

Survival

On a winter's morning the birds are silent
With puffed-up feathers
Perched on chimney tops or telephone wires
Their keen eyes searching for food.
Worms and grubs are cut off by the blanket of snow.
A door opens and an expectant flutter
Greets the thoughtful lady
Crumbs and scraps are spread.
The door closes and the birds swoop
Noisily now and anxious to get their share.
Late comers arrive
And peck for the remains.

Can you try to write your own poem called 'Survival'?

Speech marks

Each picture below gives an idea for a conversation.
Write one out using speech marks. When you have finished a
conversation, exchange it with a friend and talk about how the
speech marks were used.

The way words are built

About two thousand years ago, several tribes crossed the English Channel to settle in the island which is now called Britain. One of these tribes was called the 'Angles'. Their language was called 'Angle-ish'. This became 'English'. The name of our language, then, comes from the name of one of the tribes who spoke it.

The English spoken over a thousand years ago is known now as 'Old English'. If you looked at a piece of Old English you would not understand it at all.

The English spoken between about 400 and 900 years ago is known as 'Middle English'.
Here are four lines of a poem called 'The Knight's Tale' written by a man called Geoffrey Chaucer about 750 years ago.

To ransake in the taas of bodyes dede
Hem for to strepe of harneys and of wede
The pilours did bisyness and cure
After the bataille and disconfiture.

taas = heap
harneys = armour
wede = clothes
pilours = pillagers
cure = care
disconfiture = terrible defeat

Can you tell what the lines are about?
What makes them difficult to understand?
How many words are there which you would not have known?
With your friends, talk about how we would say the same thing today.
Try to write the four lines in modern English.

UNIT 31

Tamsin is an English girl who has been carried off into slavery in Constantinople. This city is ruled by the Turks. Dick has travelled to Constantinople in an attempt to rescue her. Dick is helped by Loukas who knows of lakes and caverns under the city. These caverns lead to a well in the courtyard of the place where Tamsin is being held.

This story is taken from a book called *The Seas of Morning* by Geoffrey Trease.

The Water Under the Earth

Loukas clambered after me, wheezing and groaning a little. He took the lantern again and led the way. At intervals there were smaller tunnels to left or right. Sometimes they brought more water, running in, but mostly they took it away to supply other parts of the city. Two or three times the rays of the lantern showed steps mounting to the world above our heads.

Once, as we passed such a staircase, the old Greek paused to listen. Faint but ominous, a long rumbling came to our ears.

'Thunder,' he said. 'I was afraid of this.'

He went forward again without further explanation. It seemed an odd moment to worry about the weather. Then I realized that, if there was a storm, it might waken the other inmates of the khan. They would think it suspicious if Tamsin went down into the courtyard in a downpour.

It was hard to guess the distance of the thunder from so far below the surface. I could only hope that the storm was over the countryside beyond the city walls.

Loukas tramped on, the lantern bobbing in his hand. The water gushed smoothly down its time-worn runnel beside us. At length he turned to speak over his shoulder.

'Not far now, sir.'

'Good!'

'We are above the ground here—we are crossing the little valley you saw.'

24

It felt just the same, though now, presumably, we were inside the aqueduct where it rode high on its arches above the roofs of the city. The thunder came clearer, but I felt more confident that it was miles away.

Again Loukas stopped. He had reached one of the small side-tunnels. It ran to the right, its arched roof barely five feet above the floor. There was no footway, but the water was only ankle-deep. It was quite still. Naturally, I told myself. At this hour nobody in the khan was likely to be drawing water, so the cistern supplying the wells must be at its normal level.

'We shall go more quietly now,' Loukas whispered. 'Voices carry a long way through these tunnels.' He began to fumble with his robe. He was divesting himself of the rope ladder, which he had carried wound round his person. 'I will give you this now, sir. I will take you to the bottom of the well. I can do no more.'

'Of course not'.

I gathered up the ladder. It was a light affair of thin cords, but it would bear my own weight easily, let alone Tamsin's. I looped it very carefully over my shoulder. The climb up the shaft was the tricky part. I could not afford to get tangled on some obstruction.

Stooping, so as not to crack our heads, we crept along the tunnel. I was so tense, I was only just aware of the icy water soaking through my shoes. Loukas stopped abruptly and I bumped into him. With a hiss of warning he raised the lantern and pointed.

We had reached the old monastery cistern. It stretched ahead into the gloom, a miniature version of the vast one we had crossed in the boat. About half a dozen simple, workaday pillars supported its vaulted roof. Loukas had explained to me, it served two other wells inside the khan. Luckily, the shaft coming down from the herb-garden was just above us. Indeed, our light revealed the rope and the bucket-handle protruding from the water.

I moved out on to a stone ledge running round the cistern wall. Loukas thrust the lantern as far as he could reach, and, looking up, I saw how the shaft narrowed overhead. As he had promised, the diameter was reasonable. An active person, who was neither too big nor too small, should be able to work his way up.

All the same, that rope would help—if I dared trust it. I stretched out my hand and managed to grip it. It was taut with the weight of that water-logged bucket at the end. I tugged cautiously. Then pulled with all my strength. It came down for another three or four feet and then resisted me. It must have reached its limit. It seemed a good tough rope,

26

and not too worn so far as my eyes and fingers could tell. But if it was going to snap, it had better snap while I was still at the bottom of the shaft, with the water to cushion my fall. I gripped it with both hands and stepped off the ledge. I found myself dangling, swinging gently to and fro. But the rope held.

There was no point in further delay. I began to climb, hand over hand. I allowed myself one glance back at Loukas. He was peering up anxiously from the curved mouth of the tunnel. Then I turned my own eyes upwards. As I left the glimmer of the lantern behind me, I could make out the pale circle of the sky.

I climbed steadily. I could hear no sound but my own heavy breathing. I was glad of the rope. Though it was not a deep well, it would have been harder work levering myself up against the rough masonry.

Not far now to the top. The sky's circle grew larger. Suddenly it brightened with a long-drawn flicker of lightning. Instinctively I glanced up again, and in that moment I saw a head silhouetted above the rim of the well. Then the thunder rolled and crashed, much nearer now.

My heart gave a wild leap. *Who* was looking down at me? If it was Tamsin, all was going unbelievably well. If it was anyone else I was done for.

Whoever it was, my presence was obviously known. I might as well find out whether it was friend or foe. I took my feet off the rope and braced them against the stonework. If it was a Turkish guard up there, he might cut the rope, and at the first sound of that I should have to let go completely and rely on arms and legs.

'Tamsin?' I called up softly.

'*Dick!*'

Even softer was the answer. It was like a sigh, but a sigh of inexpressible relief. That relief, needless to say, found its echo in my own wildly pumping heart.

In a few moments I was straddling the rim of the well. The girl's hands were helping me over. She was a dim shape in the gloom. There was not a light in the courtyard, no one else seemed to be stirring, but I could not be certain. When another lightning flash lit the sky, we should be plainly visible to any one looking out.

I had rehearsed it all in my mind. I made fast one end of the rope-ladder and let the rest of it slither quietly down into the well. Tamsin, whatever her emotions, kept wonderfully cool. She must have known, as well as I did, the folly of unnecessary words. At a touch from my hand she grasped the rope-ladder. Without hesitation, and with just the faintest rustle as her clothing brushed the stone parapet, she went over and down into the blackness.

I crouched there, alert for interruptions. But the courtyard remained silent, the surrounding buildings slept, and so—I hoped—did all the people in them.

I tested the ladder. Tamsin's weight was off. She must be safely down with Loukas. I could manage without the ladder myself, and if I left it the method of our escape would be obvious. So I unhooked it again, slipped my arm beneath the top rung, and carried it dangling from my shoulder as I went down the well-rope.

The descent seemed to take no time at all. The lantern-light came up, throwing my shadow on the wall above me. Then I was twirling round in the wider space of the vault, eager hands were clutching at me, and my feet scraped the stone ledge. I let the rope swing free and almost fell into the mouth of the tunnel. Only the restraining hand of Loukas on my shoulder saved me from straightening up and cracking my skull against its low roof.

Tamsin was clinging to me. She was sobbing now with relief. Her cheeks were wet.

A whispered warning from Loukas reminded us that this was no place to linger in. We detached ourselves. I saw now that Tamsin was dressed in the Turkish fashion, with full flowing trousers that curved down to her ankles. And round those ankles, and my own, I saw that the water in the tunnel was no longer a motionless film. It had turned into a racing rivulet, three times as deep.

'We had better go,' said Loukas gravely. 'And quickly. There must have been very heavy rain in the hills.'

He had already gathered up the rope-ladder. He led the way, and with bowed heads we went splashing after him.

The water seemed to be rising at every step. When we reached the main passage the central channel had vanished from sight. From wall to wall there was a swirling torrent. Tamsin shrank back.

'It's all right,' I shouted. 'Just keep close to the wall.'

I seized her hand and pulled her after me, and the sight of the old Greek waddling in front gave her extra reassurance. The raised walk was now itself a good twelve inches under water, but there was no danger yet, provided one did not step sideways and fall into the deeper part.

Now I realized why the thunder had troubled Loukas. He had

foreseen the threat of flood-water. I should be glad to see that boat again, waiting for us under the high vaulted roof of the Underground Palace.

I was not destined to see it.

We covered, I suppose, the first half-mile of our return journey. It was hard to measure, for the water was over our knees now and it was impossible to move fast. It was vital to keep our footing. Once swept off our feet, we might not recover ourselves.

Despite everything. Loukas was making remarkable speed for his age. I know now, stark fear was driving him. But he kept glancing back to make sure he had not lost us.

At last he waited for us. We found him high and dry on a flight of steps. 'We had better get out this way,' he panted. 'It is not ideal, but we must not risk staying in the tunnels. There may have been a cloud-burst.'

We were thankful to rest for a few minutes on those stairs. It was our first chance to talk properly.

Tamsin assured me that she was all right and fit for anything. Only later on did I fully appreciate the spirit that carried her through the ordeal of that night. It was true that she had recovered from her illness. But more recently, since learning that she had been chosen as a slave for the Serai, she had been secretly starving herself to delay the date of her being handed over.

'What now?' she demanded.

I told her.

The Venetian galley was to leave Galata at dawn, but her captain would not dare to sail with us aboard. We must join the galley only when she was safely out to sea. Loukas had fixed it. He had fishermen friends—sea fishermen. They would take us out and wait offshore for the galley, which would heave to at a signal and take us on board.

Loukas broke in. He pointed to the diminishing candle in the lantern. 'We must go, sir. We must not miss my friends. It is some way to walk. And the young lady—'He broke off, significantly. He had seen, more clearly than I had, Tamsin's weakness and weariness.

This staircase emerged into a huddle of long-abandoned ruins, lost in the undergrowth that had overwhelmed them. A nightingale was singing. There were stars in a clear sky.

Loukas extinguished his lantern. We filed forward, three shadows, along a pale ribbon of path. It brought us to one of the straight hard roads that the Romans had stretched across the city long ago.

Tamsin never uttered a murmur of complaint—indeed, nobody spoke much at all, for fear of attracting notice. It was afterwards that I was horrified, seeing her Turkish slippers worn to shreds and stuck to her feet with dried blood.

Even then, she vowed cheerfully that it was the most beautiful dawn she had ever seen in her life. Since it was the dawn of her deliverance, that was understandable.

30

To think and talk about

A 1. Who do you think had the most important part to play in the rescue of Tamsin? Give some reasons for your answer.

2. When Loukas gives Dick the ladder he says he can do no more. Why is this?

3. What tells you that Tamsin is not a weak or helpless girl?

B 1. How do you imagine Tamsin was captured?

2. Dick had been in Constantinople for some time before the rescue. How do you think he was able to enter the city and remain undetected?

3. What do you think was the most difficult and dangerous part of the venture?

4. How do you think Loukas had such a good knowledge of these underground passages?

C 1. At which point in the story would you have been most afraid? Give some reasons for your answer.

2. Imagine you are Loukas, Dick or Tamsin. What would you have done if the Turkish guards had appeared at the well?

3. Is Dick brave or foolish to get involved in this adventure? How would you describe him?

4. Which part of the whole plan do you think was most likely to fail? Give some reasons for your answer.

More books to read

1. *Popinjay Stairs* by Geoffrey Trease
   The story is set in the time of Charles II. Daniel Swift is hunting for papers which are important to the strength of the navy. You'll get an idea of this time in history as you read the story.

2. *The Wool Pack* by Cynthia Harnett
   This book won the Carnegie Medal as the best book of its year. It is about the wool trade of the Cotswolds in 1493, and should be a read to remember.

3. *On the Run* by Nina Bawden
   Ben tries to help two people who have run away from their homes. You'll find yourself caught up in the adventures that follow.

Spot the howler

That door's bolted!

The End of the Road

In these boots and with this staff
Two hundred leagues and a half
Walked I, went I, placed I, tripped I,
Marched I, held I, skelped I, slipped I,
Pushed I, panted, swung and dashed I;
Picked I, forded, swam and splashed I,
Strolled I, climbed I, crawled and scrambled,
Dropped and dipped I, ranged and rambled;
Plodded I, hobbled I, trudged and tramped I,
And in lonely spinnies camped I,
Lingered, loitered, limped and crept I,
Clambered, halted, stepped and leapt I,
Slowly sauntered, roundly strode I,
    And . . .
    Let me not conceal it . . . rode I.

Hilaire Belloc

Searching for missing words

In the passage some words have been missed out.
Can you be sure which words have been missed out?
Sometimes there can be several answers for you to think and
talk about.
How many words can you find?

The children of the village became rather a nuisance. They
would knock on his front door and ask to see the railway. Mr
Pott, once settled comfortably on the hard ground, his
wooden _____ stuck out before him, found it _____ to rise
quickly. But, being very _____ he would heave himself up and
_____ along to let in his callers. _____ would greet them
civilly, and conduct _____ down the passage, through the
_____ and out into the garden. There _____ building time was
lost in questions, _____ and general exclamation.
Sometimes, while they _____ his cement would dry, or his
_____ iron grow cold. After a time he _____ the rule that they
could only _____ at week-ends, and on Saturdays and _____
he would leave his door ajar. _____ the scullery table he set a
_____ collecting-box and the grown-ups, who now _____
were asked to pay one _____: the proceeds he sent to his
Fund. The children still came free.

From *The Borrowers Aloft* by Mary Norton

What's the truth?

Roy and Derek were sent to the headteacher for fighting in the playground.

Here is what Roy said:
'It was like this, sir, I was just playing this game. It's called hit and run. The idea is that you hit—not hard—but more tap and run. When you're caught you then have to chase. It's like tig but not quite the same. Anyway I ran past Derek and accidentally bumped into him. Then Derek went completely berserk and came after me with a piece of fencing. I had to defend myself so I took the lid from the bin. The bin lid sort of swung round and I lost my grip and it hit Derek.'

Here is Derek's account:
'I was simply minding my own business and I had this piece of fencing because I was trying to tidy up the yard. As I walked to the bin Roy attacked me from behind and knocked me to the ground. I scrambled to my feet still holding the piece of fence. It flew out of my hand and hit Roy. There was nothing I could do about it and I said sorry but Roy came at me with the bin lid. I didn't fight at all.'

How does Roy make out he is telling the truth?
Do you see any clues which suggest Derek isn't telling the truth?
What do you think **is** the truth?

The Tale of Three Landlubbers

Once upon a time three landlubbers,
Sick of the daily grind,
Aching to be free,
Leapt into a boat and braved the wintry sea.

The first, a miller (he was pale as flour),
Said:
  'I'm fed up with choking in my mill
  Hour after dusty hour.
  I'd rather be dead.'
The second, a butcher (he was lean as Spratt),
Sighed:
  'Oh for a life without a wife,
  Without the nagging and the washing up
  For breakfast, dinner, tea and sup!
  I'm for a lush and lazy clime
  And would fain grow fat.'
The third, a sweep (and he was black as night),
Cried:
  'Soot I detest!
  Not south I'd have us sail, not east nor west,
  But north to the Arctic where it's always white.'

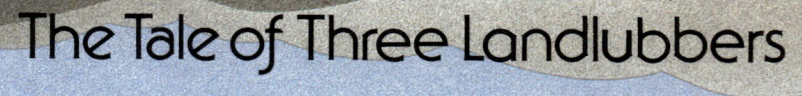

And so they sailed. Their courage sparkled bright
As the frosty stars. Their hopes were full
As the sail, high as the mountain mast,
And their hearts beat fast.
All went well—the sky was blue,
The sea calm, the cabin
Cosy as a kitten's purring.
All went well till the wind, bestirring,
Whipped up the swell and set the waves a-growling—
Down swept the tempest howling, howling.
The mast was split, the canvas rent,
The helm battered, and the oars
All of them bust or bent.
'Oh, what a mess!'
They cried. 'Back to land we go,
For there we suffered less!'
Limping, back they went.
They were lucky, though their hopes were shattered
And their courage spent.

The miller returned to his mill.
He's grinding there still.
As for the butcher, well, his wife
Was waiting for him with a stack
Of dishes, ceiling-high,
And a keen carving knife.
He went back.
He washed up.
She spared his life.
The sweep returned to his soot
And his dreams of the Arctic white.
He's black again from morn to night,
From head to foot.

And they all stayed put.

Ian Serraillier

How to use a book

You are doing a project on time and want to find:
1. When our present calendar was first used.
2. How the days of the week got their names.
Skim the following passage quickly to find the information you are looking for.

The calendar in its present form has only been in force for just over 200 years. In 1752, when the new calendar came into use, the day after September 2nd was September 14th—and people who thought they had lost eleven days of their lives protested violently.

However, the alteration was necessary because Julius Caesar, on the advice of an astronomer, counted the year as 365¼ days, and arranged his calendar accordingly. Unfortunately, he was just over 11 minutes out (the year is in fact 365 days 5 hours 48 minutes 46 seconds long) and by the time his calendar had been in use 1500 years these minutes had added up to 10 days! Pope Gregory therefore put things right in 1582, by dropping 10 days between October 4th and 15th. He also arranged that although 1600 would be a leap year, neither 1700, 1800 nor 1900 should be. The English did not adopt this calendar till nearly 200 years later. Although the present calendar is so recent, the names of the months and days go back much further. Most of the English names of the days are derived from those given them by the Saxons and Danes, while the months have Roman names. September, October, November and December were originally the 7th, 8th, 9th and 10th months, as their names indicate, and July and August were named after Julius and Augustus Caesar.

Look up any encyclopaedia you may have in your class and skim quickly to find the following facts.
1. The day and date when the Second World War began.
2. The year in which Leonardo Da Vinci was born.
Pick any other topic in your encyclopaedia. Skim quickly a short section and look for four or five facts which you think are important.

Read and remember

Can you read carefully and remember what you've read?
Here is a short story. Read it carefully and try to remember the events as they are told in the story.
Do you think you'll remember when you turn to page 43?

The Fair

The fair had come to town. After school Sally and Pete rushed down to the common to watch them putting up the roundabouts, the helter skelter, the shooting gallery, and all the other side shows. Music was already pouring out when they arrived and dozens of people were rushing about busily.

They saw two men carrying a huge board with 'Ghost Train' and a black skull painted on it. A woman was arranging the targets in the shooting range and another was setting out the prizes—pink teddy bears, brightly painted plates, and shining brass vases. Two children were helping by fitting the light bulbs around the outside.

It all seemed so exciting and strange. Sally and Pete thought it would be much more fun to live with the fair than at home. 'I bet they don't have to go to school,' Sally whispered.

Imagine her surprise the next day when the two children appeared in her classroom. The teacher introduced them and explained that they would be staying for a week while the fair was in town. At break the children gathered round them excitedly asking about life with the fair.

'Do you get free turns on all the rides?'
'Do you live in a caravan?'
'Do you have to move every week?'
'What about your friends?'
Sally began to think that life with the fair wasn't all fun.

Now turn to page 43.

To talk and write about

1. Imagine you are either Tamsin or Dick.
   Write a diary account of your adventures.
   If you choose to be Tamsin begin with your capture.
   If you choose to be Dick begin with your setting sail from Venice.

2. 'Over Asia the sky brightened. Domes and minarets stood black against it. Water glistened. The Sea of Marmara, glimpsed above the walls.'
   In a few sentences the author gives a picture of dawn.
   Talk about how you would describe dawn breaking.
   Here is how Mark began his description:
   > 'At first we couldn't make out anything. There was only a distant glow to tell us the sun would soon burst forth to start a new day.'

   Try to give a clear description of how you can see more and more objects or people as the light increases.

Reading for the main idea

Have a close look at this main idea 'tree' which Nadya made.

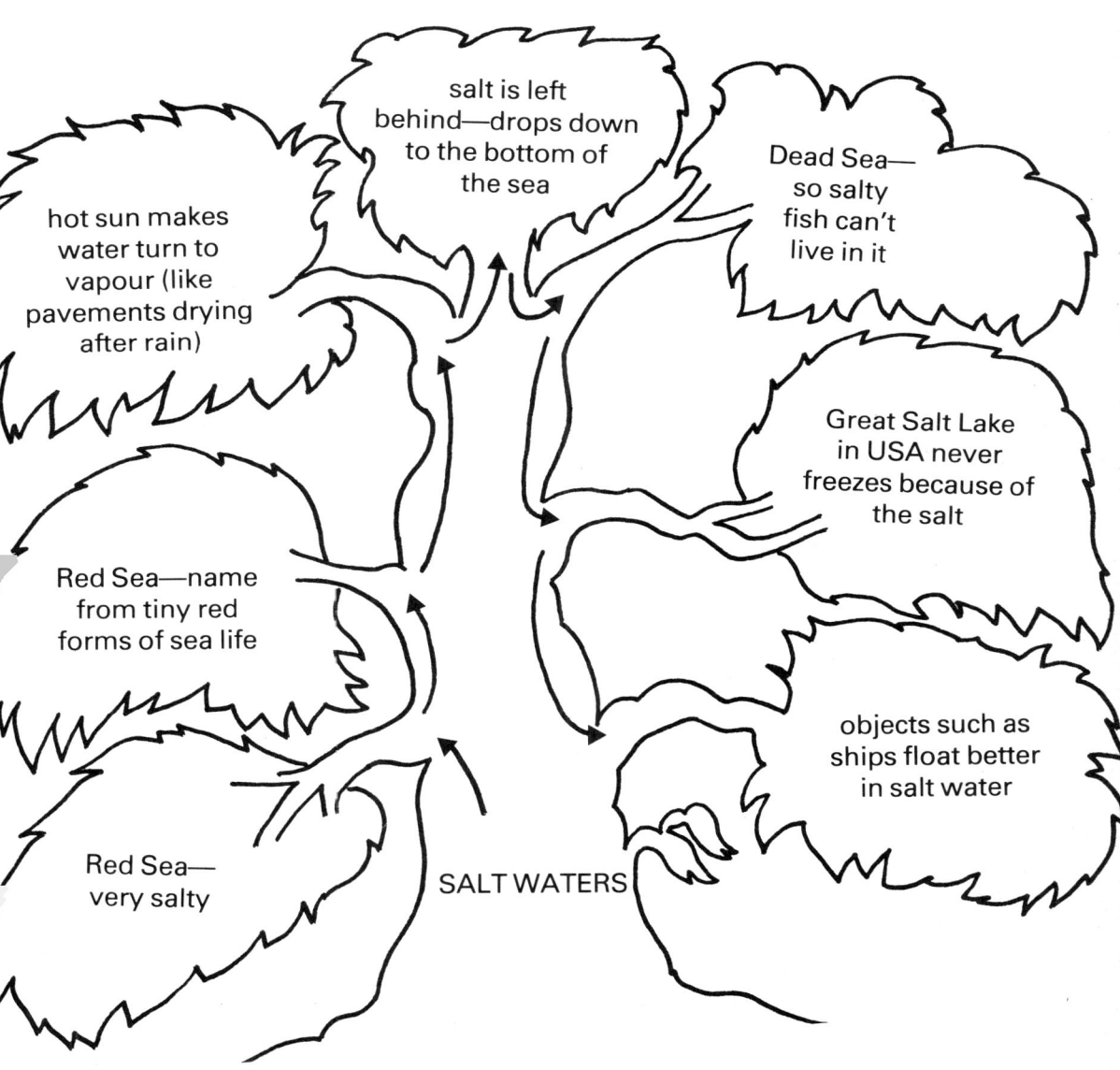

salt is left behind—drops down to the bottom of the sea

Dead Sea—so salty fish can't live in it

hot sun makes water turn to vapour (like pavements drying after rain)

Great Salt Lake in USA never freezes because of the salt

Red Sea—name from tiny red forms of sea life

objects such as ships float better in salt water

Red Sea—very salty

SALT WATERS

Can you use Nadya's 'tree' to write a short passage about salt waters?

Using a dictionary

1. Look up each word in bold type below in your dictionary. Which meaning from the dictionary is being used in each sentence?

   bear
   (a) Mother said she could hardly **bear** to cut the beautiful cake.
   (b) Next autumn we expect our plans to **bear** fruit.
   (c) This steel beam will **bear** the entire weight of the building, until it is complete.

   credit
   (a) I can scarcely **credit** that you could have been so stupid.
   (b) Winnie is a **credit** to us all, having worked so hard.
   (c) I found that I had less to my **credit** at the bank than I thought.

   pitch
   (a) 'Here, mate, this is my **pitch**', said the match-seller, 'so just you move on.'
   (b) A writer of school books has to **pitch** the work at the right level of difficulty for the children who will use the book.
   (c) There was a single shot, and Harrison **pitched** forward onto his face.

2. Which of the three words in brackets is the best one to fit the sentence? If you can answer these questions without a large dictionary, you are probably a genius!

   (a) The undertaker entered the room, his (**physiognomic, lugubrious, avuncular**) face seeming constantly on the verge of tears.
   (b) It is most unwise to (**contravene, contradict, institute**) this law, as you could face a large fine.
   (c) Children are thought to (**constitute, countenance, decapitate**) the greater part of the market for this product.
   (d) Gavin is a (**myopic, overwrought, loquacious**) child if ever there was, for he simply cannot keep his mouth shut.

42

Read and remember

Can you put the sentences below in the same order as in the story 'The Fair' on page 39?
Don't look back to the story.

(a) Two children from the fair appeared in Sally's school one morning.

(b) They watched two men carrying a huge board with 'Ghost Train' and a black skull painted on it.

(c) Sally and Pete rushed down to watch the fair being put up after school.

(d) Two children were helping by putting light bulbs round the shooting range.

(e) Sally and Pete thought it would be fun to live with the fair.

Funny words

What word do you think the artist has drawn in this picture?

There are lots of words which are funny if you think about them. Talk about how you might make a funny drawing of the word.

kneecap

Can you draw a picture for **kneecap**?

To talk and write about

As Dick climbed the rope the author describes his fear.
'I glanced up again, and in that moment I saw a head silhouetted above the rim of the well. Then the thunder rolled and crashed much nearer now. My heart gave a wild leap.'
When he realised it was Tamsin the author describes Dick's relief like this:
'It was a sigh, but a sigh of inexpressible relief. The relief found its echo in my wildly pumping heart.'
Talk about these descriptions of fear.

Look at this picture.

Imagine you are faced with this group.
Describe the fear that you feel as you approach.
Are your fears well founded or are the figures friends?
Describe the scene and add more details as it becomes more obvious who is awaiting you.

What did they say?

Harry talks to the school caretaker.

I'm trying to find out about the people who make our school run smoothly. What do you think is the most important part of your job, Mr Lee?

Well, Harry, I think the most important things are the security of the school and arranging for the building to be kept clean.

What exactly do you mean by security?

Well, the school has a lot of valuable things in it, like tape recorders and televisions which criminals might want to steal. I have to make sure that the buiding is properly locked up.

How many cleaners are there in the school?

There are three cleaners.

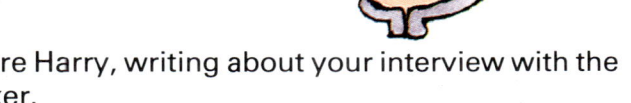

Imagine you are Harry, writing about your interview with the school caretaker.
Start like this:

> I started by telling Mr Lee that I was trying to find out about the people who make our school run smoothly. I asked him what the most important part of his . . .

Can you finish the report?

Act it out

With some friends, act this scene.
Four people are the only survivors of a shipwreck.
They are on a liferaft which can only take three.
One must get off in order to save the others.
None is willing to, so it is decided to find who is the least important in life.
Each of you must decide who you are and try to persuade the others why you must be allowed to live.
Who will win?

Beginnings

The answer to each of the five clues starts with the same letters.
Each answer is a word. The beginning letters are given in capitals.
Use your dictionary to find the answers.

SUB
- **split into smaller parts**
- **sink down**
- **put something in place of another thing**
- **under the sea**
- **large**

How on earth!

Talk about the strange scene in the picture.
How might it have happened?
Could you write a story about it?

46

The way words are built

About four hundred years ago, people from Britain started to move to other parts of the world to live. Because they spoke English, the language is now found in all parts of the world where they settled.

However, English-speaking people in different parts of the world have their own ways of saying things. Below is a list of English phrases from different parts of the world. There is also a list of the countries they are used in, but it is mixed up. Can you say which phrase comes from which country?

Stone the crows!	New Zealand
I'm a-fixin' to do that.	England
'Ere, give over!	USA
Away and no haver!	Australia
She'll be right!	Scotland

Can you say what each one means?
Can you find other phrases in your part of the world which you think are not used in other places?
How would you be able to tell?
Have you any relatives who live far away?
Do they say things which you think are strange? What things?

UNIT 32

The story of Beowulf was written over a thousand years ago, in the language which we now call Old English. In this part, Beowulf, a great hero, is having a desperate battle with a terrible monster.

Rosemary Sutcliff wrote *Dragon Slayer* which is based on Beowulf, and our story comes from this.

Battle With the Sea Hag

Down and down sank Beowulf into the cold swinging depths; down and down for what seemed the whole of a day. From all sides the tusked sea beasts rushed in upon him, striving to gore him to pieces; and ever as he sank he fought them off with stroke and lunge of the great sword Hrunting. At last his feet touched the sea floor, and instantly an enemy far more dire was upon him, as the Sea-Hag leapt to fling her arms about him, clutching him to her with claws as terrible as her son's had been. He was being rushed through the black depths, close-locked in her dreadful embrace, and now, still together, they were diving upward through the under-water mouth of a cave.

Up and up . . . They were in a vast sea-hall above the tide line, white sand underfoot, and the faint light of day falling in shafts from some opening to the clifftop far above. Beowulf tore himself free and springing clear for a sword stroke, brought Hrunting whistling down on her head. The cave rang with the blow, but for the first time since it was forged the blade refused to bite, and next instant she was upon him once more. He stumbled beneath her onslaught and she flung him down with herself on top of him, stabbing again and again at his breast with her saex, her broad-bladed dagger, and when that failed to pierce his battle-sark clawing and worrying at him as though she were a wolf indeed. He saw her fangs sharp behind her snarling lips, and her eyes shone with balefire amid the tangle of her hair; but the ring-mail of the Queen's gift withstood her still, and gathering his strength he flung her off a second time, and springing up, aimed at her a blow that should have swept her head from her shoulders.

Again her charmed hide turned the stroke; and with a cry he flung the useless weapon aside. 'Come then, my naked hands shall serve me as they served me in the hall of Hrothgar!' and he sprang to meet her next attack.

49

There on the silver sand, with the roar of the sea echoing about them hollow like the echo in a vast shell, he with one arm locked about her and the other straining at her dagger wrist, she striving always with fang and claw to come at his heart, they reeled and trampled to and fro, as two nights since he had reeled and trampled to and fro with Grendel in the darkened hall of Heorot.

Long and bitter was the struggle, but there was a strength in the Sea-Hag that had not been in her son, and Beowulf could not overcome it. Some weapon he must have, and as he fought he snatched desperate glances about him in search of one. Here and there ancient weapons hung on the rock walls of the cavern, and among them the light from the roof fell upon one sword, a huge sword, dwarf-wrought perhaps for giants in the far-past days, for it was so long in the blade and broad in the grip that no mortal man save Beowulf could have wielded it. Seeing it, his heart leapt up with fresh hope, and gathering all his strength and cunning he gave way before the Sea-Hag's onslaught, then swerved and sprang sideways past her, to snatch it from the wall. His hand closed over the hilt, and with a triumphant battle-shout he whirled around and brought the blade down upon her in a flashing swoop of fire.

It shored through hair and hide and bone, and Grendel's Dam dropped without a sound, her hideous head all but smitten from her shoulders.

Beowulf stood still, panting from his struggle, and looked about him, while the magic blade dripped red in his hand. Far off at the water's edge, the light from the upper world showed him the gigantic body of Grendel lying outstretched, dead, and he strode towards it across the stained and trampled sand. Here at last, it seemed, he had a blade that could pierce the flesh of Grendel and his kin, and raising it once more with a mighty effort he smote loathsome head and loathsome body asunder. Blood streamed out into the water in a murky crimson flood that the sea sucked under and out through the mouth of the cave. And as Beowulf stood gazing down at the dead monster, the thick dark blood dripping along the blade ate into it and melted it away like ice in the warmth of a fire, until nothing was left but the wondrous gold-wrought hilt in his hand.

Then Beowulf stooped and twisted his free hand in the snaky hair of the severed head, and with the sword hilt still in the other, dived down to the cave mouth and triumphantly up through the water that was now clear and bright; up and up towards the daylight far above him.

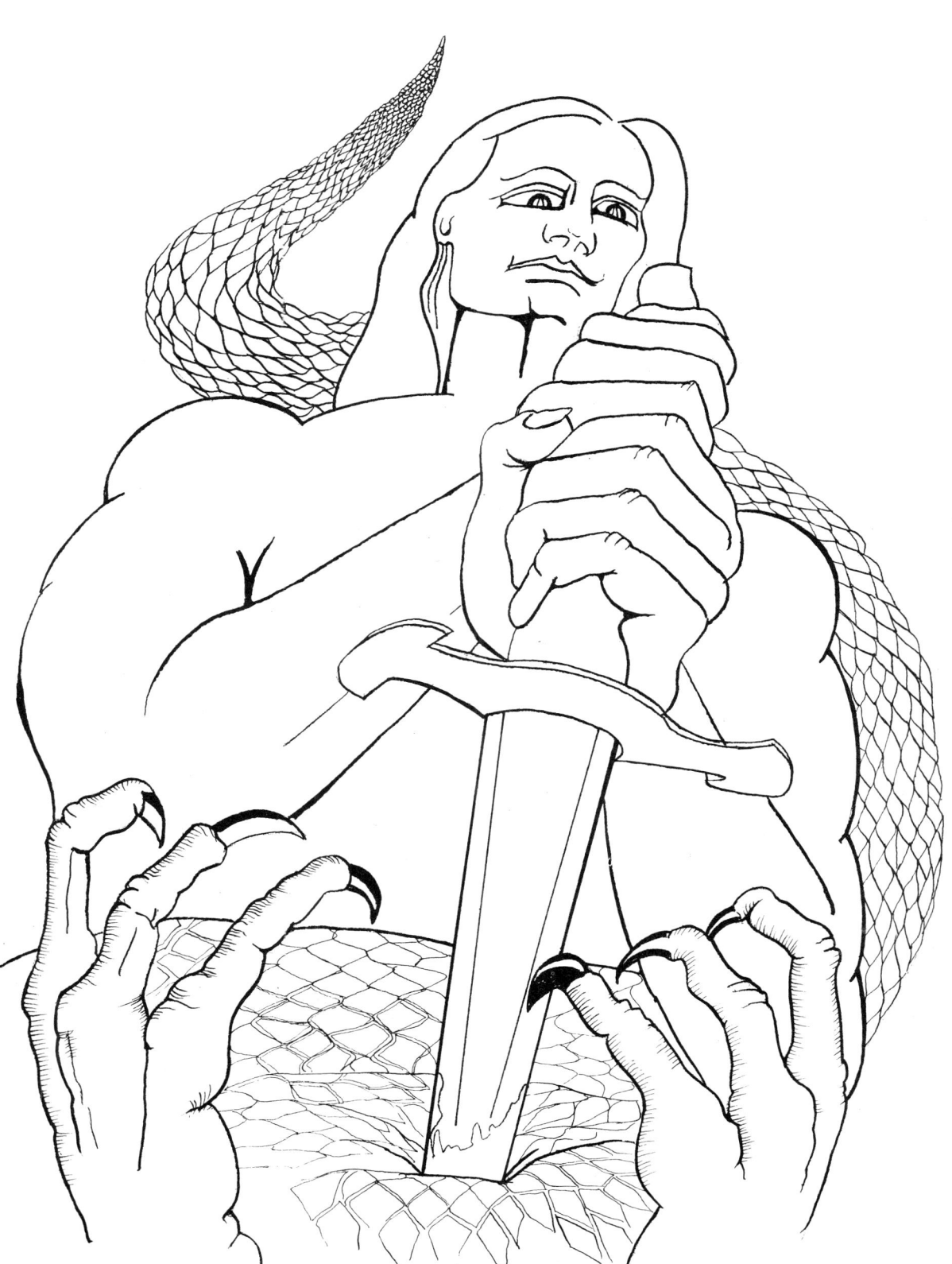

To think and talk about

A 1. Why is the Hag so difficult to overcome?

   2. What advantages would you say Beowulf had on his side?

   3. Do you think Beowulf is good at hand-to-hand combat?

   4. From what we learn of him, what sort of man is Beowulf?

B 1. Why do you think swords were given names?

   2. Where do you think the weapons hanging in the Sea Hag's cavern have come from?

   3. The things we believe in and know about are different in many ways from those things which people 1000 years ago knew and believed in. How much of this story do you think the people of 1000 years ago would have believed?

   4. Why do you think the author chose the sea for this scene?

C 1. Imagine you are Beowulf. What are your thoughts during the fight? Was there a point at which you thought you might lose?

   2. Imagine you are the Sea Hag. What are your thoughts during the fight? What are your dying thoughts?

   3. Was there anything about the way the story was written which you particularly liked or disliked? Why?

   4. Did you enjoy the story? Why?

More books to read

1. *Horned Helmet* by Henry Treece
   The story of Beorn an Icelandic boy who runs away from his master and is helped by Starkad the fearful Jomsviking. Exciting reading.

2. *The Eagle of the Ninth* by Rosemary Sutcliff
   Marcus becomes a spy in hostile territory so that he can clear his father's name by finding the lost Eagle of the Ninth Legion. You should find this a gripping story.

3. *No Way of Telling* by Emma Smith
   Amy and her grandmother were in a mountain cottage. A blizzard raged. Suddenly the door burst open and a figure more like a monster than a man burst in, grabbed some food and disappeared. You'll find it difficult to put this story down until you find out what happens.

To write about

One day you are out walking with a friend, and in a pond you see the glint of metal. On reaching into the water, you find that there is a sword hilt, which seems to be made of gold, and is intricately carved. While you are examining it, the sun reflects from the gold into your eyes, and suddenly you are transported in time. The hilt is suddenly a whole sword, iron blade gleaming. Before you stands a hideous monster . . .

Write the story of what happens.

Searching for missing words

In the passage some words have been missed out.
Can you be sure which words have been missed out?
Sometimes there can be only one answer.
Sometimes there can be several answers for you to think and
talk about.
How many words can you find?

Boggis and Toseland paddled off side by side across the drive
and turned into a walled yard that was now a walled lake,
though you could see the cobbles through the shallow water,
all different colours like pebbles at the sea-side. Along three
sides there were buildings or sheds, very _____ and
tumbledown. The longest had a _____ of arches, and over
them bits of _____ stone carving stuck out of the _____.
Inside it was divided up into _____ rooms with scrolled iron
doorways opening _____ to a passage. Some were filled
_____ straw, some with faggots or peat. _____ was empty,
and one had a _____ ladder with hand and foot holes _____ of
rungs. Up this Boggis went _____ through a trap-door above.
   Tolly _____, and found himself in a room _____ like his
bedroom but much larger, _____ of hay and sawdust and rich
_____ a soft, musty kind of darkness.

From *The Children of Green Knowe* by Lucy Boston

/

54

What's the truth?

Jim, of the *Daily View* and Brenda, of the *Weekly Round-Up*, went to see the first showing of the film 'Sheriff Baines'.

Here is what Jim wrote about the film:
The action of the film developed carefully to the crisis point when Sheriff Baines was told to get out of town by the very people who employed him. The tension at that point was heightened by superb acting and the viewer will be exhausted trying to determine whether or not Sheriff Baines will win through. The film ends with a marvellous shoot-out in which the clever tactics of Baines are successful. Not a film for those who are a bit nervous.

Brenda said this of the film:
If you're feeling tired and can't sleep, go and see 'Sheriff Baines.' The story took so long to build up I thought we would never get there. Unfortunately it was obvious after five minutes that the film would end in a big shoot out. How Baines escaped the bullets which rained down on him was unbelievable. However, the film was helped along by some good acting, that is the acting I managed to take in between nodding off for forty winks. The scenery was good.

What words does Jim use to show he likes the film?
How do you know Brenda didn't like the film?
Can they both be right?

The Bear

His sullen shaggy-rimmed eyes followed my
   every move.
Slowly gyrating they seemed to mimic the
   movements of his massive head.
Similarly his body rolled unceasingly
From within.
As though each part possessed its own motion
And could think
And could move for itself alone.
He had come forward in a lumbering, heavy spurt;
Like a beer barrel rolling down a plank.
The tremendous volume of his blood-red mouth
Yawned
So casually
But with so much menace.
And still the eye held yours.
So that you had to stay.
And then it turned.
Away.
So slowly.
Back
With that same motion
Back
To the bun strewn
And honey-smelling back of its cage.

Frederick Brown

Is it in the passage?

Leo and Zoe were interested in forming a rock climbing club for juniors and wrote this letter to their school magazine.

Dear Editor,

Our rock-climbing club is looking for new junior members. Before you rush, however, be warned! We're fit, sensible, good-natured people who like the outdoor life. Thus, before you can join, you have to pass some difficult tests to show that you are capable enough to join our group. You will also be required to pay a joining fee to provide all the necessary equipment. If you still think you meet the description please contact us. It's an expensive hobby but provides great excitement and adventure. You'll meet interesting people, see fabulous new sights and build up new confidence in yourself!

Yours faithfully,
Leo and Zoe

Read the sentences below and then put them into three groups:
- (a) Facts which are in the passage
- (b) Opinions which are in the passage
- (c) Fact or opinions which are *not* in the passage.

1. Not everyone will be allowed to join the club.
2. You must have plenty of money before you can join the club.
3. Rock climbing keeps people fit.
4. Zoe and Leo are intelligent and good natured.
5. If you join the club you'll find excitement and adventure.
6. Those who join have to pay a fee.
7. Rock climbing is an extremely dangerous occupation.
8. If you think you meet the requirements you are to contact Leo and Zoe.
9. Rock climbers are warned not to rush up mountains.
10. Rock climbing builds self confidence.

Sort it out

This exercise is really difficult!
Here is a story which Julie wrote about the first car her father owned.
The paragraphs are in the wrong order.
The sentences in each paragraph are in the wrong order.
Can you sort the story out, so that it makes sense?
First sort out the sentences in each paragraph.
Then sort out the paragraphs.

1. (a) Although it was old, it was in very good condition.

   (b) When Dad bought it, it had had several owners, and was already quite old.

   (c) It was very reliable, and never once let us down.

   (d) The car was a Morris Minor.

2. (a) He got out the rope, hitched it up to our little old Morris, and towed it ten miles to the nearest garage!

   (b) The other car was large, shiny, and almost brand new.

   (c) The first was a drive in the country when we came across another car, broken down.

   (d) Weren't we proud of our old car!

   (e) Dad stopped, but he found that the car would not start.

   (f) So what did he do?

3. (a) A part of my life went that day.

   (b) It was a sad day when the old Morris went on its last journey.

   (c) We all watched as Dad drove it away to the scrapyard, still running perfectly.

   (d) Although the engine was good, the body had become dangerously rusty.

   (e) We all loved the old car, but now it had to go.

   (f) It had become too expensive to be worth keeping.

4. (a) After that there were many trips I could tell you about, but two stand out in my mind.

   (b) I suppose I must have been four.

   (c) My earliest memory of the old Morris is being sick on its back seat after a trip to the seaside.

5. (a) He kept it for a long time, and I have many happy memories of it.

   (b) When I was two, Dad bought a car.

   (c) I would like to tell you something about it.

6. (a) There were the four of us plus my Aunt and Uncle.

   (b) The boot was crammed full.

   (c) We had a marvellous holiday.

   (d) The good old car travelled the two hundred miles with this huge load as if it were nothing.

   (e) We had all our camping gear tied to the roof rack.

   (f) Another time we went camping on the coast.

A Small Dragon

I've found a small dragon in the woodshed.
Think it must have come from deep inside a forest
because it's damp and green and leaves
are still reflecting in its eyes.

I fed it on many things, tried grass,
the roots of stars, hazel-nut and dandelion,
but it stared up at me as if to say, I need
foods you can't provide.

It made a nest among the coal,
not unlike a bird's but larger,
it is out of place here
and is quite silent.

If you believed in it I would come
hurrying to your house to let you share my wonder,
but I want instead to see
if you yourself will pass this way.

Brian Patten

Reading for the main idea

Colin was working on a project about **homes** and came across this passage in a book.

Long ago people made their homes in places which gave them shelter and safety from the wild animals that roamed the earth. Some lived in or among trees where they were high above ground and safe from prowling animals or flooding. Others lived in caves which they heated by making fires. Later, people learned to make their own types of shelter like tents or huts. Tents were useful, when tribes of people moved on to new ground following herds of wild animals which they hunted for food and clothing, as they could be dismantled and taken with them. Once people had learned to grow food and farm, more permanent homes were needed. These huts would be made using any available materials found nearby. Stone was good because it is strong and able to keep out wind and rain. Turf and animals skins were often used to make them less draughty and living together in one room also helped to heat the dwelling.

Colin made notes of the main ideas in the story and also wanted notes of important details. He arranged his main ideas and notes as shown below. Can you add the other main ideas and make a 'tree' of your own?

safe from flooding (tree house)

from wild animals

for shelter and safety

HOMES

To talk and write about

How old do you expect to be when you die?
How old is the oldest person you know?
In the days when the story of Beowulf was written, someone
who reached the age of forty was lucky, for most people died
before they reached that age.
There was no medicine, and the real 'monsters' which killed
were illness and disease.
What are the 'monsters' of the twentieth century?
The pictures below may give you some ideas.

Talk about the photos. What is each one showing? In what way
may each be said to be a 'monster'? Can you add any?
Find out all you can about the things shown in these pictures.
Write a report called 'Monsters of the Modern Age.'

WARNING

OIL ON
BEACH

AMBULANCE

Billy Scoop, ace reporter from the *Daily Report*, a local newspaper in the town where the school was on fire, spoke to various people there. Below is what two of them said, and the questions they were asked.

First is Mrs Watson, the Headteacher.

Scoop: When were you first told about the fire?
Mrs Watson: I had just gone to bed when the phone rang. It was the caretaker, Mr Edwards. I came straight here.
Scoop: The fire seems to have quite a hold. If the building is completely destroyed, what will the children do for a school?
Mrs Watson: It is a bit early to say, but the education authority will doubtless be able to make some arrangements.

Next, Mr Edwards, the caretaker.

Mr Edwards: This is terrible, terrible, I told them years ago that I thought there was a fault in that boiler . . .
Scoop: So you think you know what may have caused the fire?
Mr Edwards: It could be something else, but I have suspected an electrical fault in the boiler that runs the central heating for some time.
Scoop: Perhaps the children will get an extra holiday?
Mr Edwards: Well, there won't be a school for them to go to, not here at any rate . . .

Talk about how Scoop will go about writing his report for the next day's paper.
Here is the beginning of the report.

SCHOOL INFERNO
Our local school at Ruston was destroyed by fire late last night. Our reporter on the scene talked to the caretaker . . .

Finish the report.

To write about

1. Imagine that you are a newspaper reporter who has waited for an interview with Beowulf after the fight with the Sea Hag. Think of the questions you would ask him. What answers do you think he would give?
Write the report you would send to your newspaper.
Start with this headline.

   BEOWULF DOES IT AGAIN!

2. Do you think the people of 1000 years ago had reasons for believing in monsters like Grendel, and the Sea Hag? Find out about these monsters, which even now, people are not sure about:

   the Loch Ness Monster
   the Yeti.

   Write a report called 'Monsters—Fact or Fiction?'

The way words are built

An Interesting Surname

Singh is a common surname among Sikhs. It has an interesting story.

In the seventeenth century, the people of the Sikh religion in Asia found themselves under attack from their enemies. As a symbol of the strength and courage the Sikhs had to show, their leader at that time adopted the title of 'Singh' which means 'a lion'. Since then the Sikhs have always included this among their names.

Act it out

You have taken your dog for a walk in the park.
The dog has gone for a swim in the duckpond and will not come out.
Act the scene of yourself on the bank, trying to persuade your (imaginary) dog to come out of the pond, without getting wet yourself.

The company words keep

It is difficult to believe that the lion and the kitten are related, isn't it?

Make a list of words you would use to describe the lion.

Ian thought of these to start you off.

regal   **proud**   **dangerous**   **unapproachable**

Now do the same for the kitten.

Ian thought of these to start you off.

playful   **clumsy**   **comic**   **bright**

Use your lists of words to write a description of each animal.

Ian *started* his description like this—

The huge lion sat in the dust, his regal head raised.
His proud eyes gazed balefully in my direction,
daring me to approach within striking distance.

Make your descriptions as full as possible.

Mr Corvo has been on trial and the jury have found him not guilty. The judge, however, Mr Justice Rumple, doesn't like the verdict and has imprisoned the jury along with Mr Corvo!

This is the story of how Dorinda and Dinah persuade Mr Justice Rumple to change his mind and free Mr Corvo and the jury.

This story is taken from a book called *The Wind on the Moon* by Eric Linklater.

Change Your Mind!

'Do you remember,' said Dorinda after breakfast, 'that quite a long time ago, before Father had gone abroad, we went down to the river, and I happened to have a fork, and we caught two eels?'

'And put them in a bottle that we found,' said Dinah.

'And then put a cork in the bottle, to prevent them from getting out.'

'And took the bottle home, and left it behind the tool-shed, and then we forgot all about it.'

'The eels must be dead by now,' said Dorinda.

'Horribly dead,' said Dinah thoughtfully. 'It was very naughty of us, but all the same they may be useful.'

'That's just what I was thinking.'

'And the three kippers that we bought yesterday are beginning to smell already.'

'We've got all we need now except the postcards,' said Dorinda, 'and we can write them while we're doing our lessons.'

In the afternoon they walked over the fields to Mr. Justice Rumple's house on the other side of the river. They avoided Midmeddlecum, because they were carrying several parcels which they did not wish to be seen. They had chosen the proper time to arrive—the time when the Judge, with his Cook and his Tablemaid and his Housemaid, usually went out to have a game of clock-golf—and because the dining-room window was wide open, and the sill no more than two feet from the ground, they got in quite easily, without anyone seeing them, and without having to ring the bell or knock at the door.

70

Then, quietly and quickly, they went upstairs and found the Judge's bedroom. They knew it was his, because on a table in a corner there were three busts of Caesar and Shakespeare and the Duke of Wellington, and each of them was wearing one of the Judge's spare wigs.

'And now,' said Dinah, 'what do you want to do with the mice?'

'Come here,' said Dorinda, who had crawled under the bed, and when Dinah followed her, she pointed to the spiral springs on which the mattress rested.

'They look rather like little cages, don't they?' she asked. 'It would be a very appropriate place to put mice, and nobody will ever think of looking for them there.'

Dinah agreed, so they pushed the six dead field-mice into six of the spiral springs that supported the Judge's bed, and crawling from under it, looked through the window at the lawn where the Judge was playing clock-golf with his Cook, his Tablemaid, and his Housemaid. Then they set to work again.

'This must be his dressing-room,' said Dinah, opening another door.

'What a lot of clothes he has!' said Dorinda, looking into a wardrobe.

'And dozens and dozens of shirts,' said Dinah, examining a chest of drawers.

Some of the postcards which they had written were concealed in the neat array of shirts, and others thrust into the pockets of his various suits, and when that was done Dinah said they must look for the library.

That was on the ground floor, and as soon as they went in they saw, on a very ornamental marble mantelpiece, two tall Greek vases of the sort which Miss Serendip had taught them to call an amphora.

'The very thing!' said Dinah, and drawing a chair to the mantelpiece she climbed up, and having pulled the cork from the bottle containing the dead eels, she hid it in the nearer vase.

'Isn't it horrible!' cried Dorinda, as she sniffed the dreadful smell that came from the uncorked bottle.

'It's worse than horrible,' said Dinah. 'If that doesn't make him change his mind, nothing will.'

'And we still have the kippers,' said Dorinda.

'I think the dining-room is the proper place for them. You remember those enormous oil-paintings which are probably his father and his mother? And another, of sheep walking over a mountain? We could pin the kippers to the wall behind them with these drawing-pins that I brought.'

Dorinda had no better suggestion to make, so that was quickly done, and they left the house through the open dining-room window, and walked into Midmeddlecum. They wanted to see Catherine Crumb, the baker's daughter.

They both heartily disliked Catherine, with her wicked face and her long thin legs, and they had by no means forgiven her for what she had once done to them when, after eating too much, they had swollen into something very like balloons. But they knew that Catherine was the most useful person in the village for their present purpose, because she had a natural gift for mischief and loved nothing better.

She was very much surprised, and rather frightened, when they arrived at her house and told her they had something very secret to talk about. But no sooner had they explained their plan to her, and described what they had done already, and made clear what they wanted her to do, than her wicked face grew pale with excitement, her dark eyes gleamed with pleasure, and she pulled the joints of her fingers so that each of them made a noise like a stick breaking.

'You can depend on me,' she promised. 'All the children here will do what I tell them, and if the Judge doesn't change his mind within a week, you can stick more pins in me than I ever stuck into you.'

'Thank you,' said Dinah, a trifle haughtily, 'but we never stick pins in people.'

'Don't if you don't want to,' said Catherine. 'It won't make any difference to what I've promised.'

Then for a day or two Dinah and Dorinda waited impatiently to see how their plan was going to work, and before long they had very good news of it. The Judge was beginning to look thoroughly unhappy, and his Cook reported that he had entirely lost his appetite.

After finishing his game of clock-golf, on the afternoon when Dinah and Dorinda left the mice and the eels and the kippers in his house, the Judge had gone into the library to read, and was immediately aware of a strange smell in the room. So he rang the bell and the Tablemaid came in, and when he told her to sniff she sniffed, and looked rather surprised, but answered, 'I smell nothing but your cigar.'

Then he rang for the Housemaid and made her sniff. 'I smell nothing but the nice leather smell of your armchair,' she said.

Then the Judge, growing angry, sent for the Cook, and made her sniff all round the room like a bloodhound. But the Cook, in a very determined voice, said, 'I smell nothing but that bowl of lovely roses,

which I cut for you myself, and which I myself put on your desk.'

The truth was that all of them could smell the strange odour in the room, but none would admit it, because they worked very hard to keep the house tidy and clean, and they refused to believe there could be anything dirty or out of place in it.

So the Judge sent them away and tried to persuade himself that the smell was nothing but imagination, and after an hour or two he became used to it and did not notice it. But on the following morning, going to breakfast in the dining-room, he sniffed and sniffed, and summoning again his Cook and his Tablemaid and his Housemaid, declared, 'There is a disgusting smell in this room also. What is it, what causes it, and why do you permit it?'

But all of them, looking very smart and clean in their print dresses and white aprons, with their faces newly washed, indignantly replied that the room smelt sweet as a garden, and always would while the house was in their charge. So the Judge ate his breakfast unhappily and went out quickly. But on his way through Midmeddlecum he passed several little boys and several little girls who, when they saw him coming, hurriedly avoided him and held their noses in a very ostentatious way.

The smell in the library was much worse that evening, and when he went to bed he lay awake for at least an hour, sniffing from time to time, and saying to himself, 'It is only imagination. It can be nothing but imagination.'

In the morning, however, the smell of mouse was undeniable, and rising early he searched the room for the source of it, but found nothing. He did find, however, in the folds of a clean shirt, a postcard on which was written:

HAVE YOU CHANGED YOUR MIND TO-DAY?

This made him very angry, but as soon as he went into the dining-room he felt more worried than angry for by now the room was smelling unmistakably of bad fish. Quickly he felt for his handkerchief—and found in his pocket another postcard with the inscription:

HAVE YOU CHANGED YOUR MIND TO-DAY?

In Midmeddlecum that morning at least thirty little boys and girls, in the most pointed manner, held their noses while he passed, and twice he heard Catherine Crumb explaining to them in her shrill voice: 'He hasn't changed his mind for weeks and weeks!'

74

This state of affairs lasted for several days, and the Judge grew more and more worried, and the several odours of mice and kippers and eels grew worse and worse in his house, for though the Cook and the Tablemaid and the Housemaid dusted and cleaned from morning till night, and searched again and again for the source of the smell, they never thought of looking in the springs under the bed, or in the Greek amphora, or behind the paintings of the Judge's father and mother. So in a few days' time he became thin and haggard, and wherever he went he heard voices saying, 'He hasn't changed his mind for weeks and weeks!' He began to wonder whether that indeed was the cause of all the disagreeable odours in his house.

And then one night he could not sleep at all, for the smell of mouse was stronger than ever, and the dining-room had smelt abominably of fish, and the smell of decay in the library had been perfectly disgusting. He sat up in bed and turned on the light, and looked at his watch. It was four o'clock. Quite soon he would have to get up, and walk into Midmeddlecum, where all the little boys and girls would hold their noses when they saw him coming, and ostentatiously avoid him.

'Oh, what shall I do, what shall I do?' he exclaimed, and tore a strip off the top sheet before he realised what he *was* doing.

Then he seemed to hear a mysterious voice say to him: 'Tearing sheets won't help you, what you've got to do is to change your mind. *Change your mind.* CHANGE YOUR MIND!'

A hundred and fifty-seven times the voice repeated its message, and then the Judge lost his temper and shouted, 'All right, all right. I heard you the first time! I'll change it, if that's the only way to get rid of these confounded smells. I'll change it, I tell you, but give me a chance! I've got to get my trousers on first.'

He got up and dressed as quickly as he could, and walked through Midmeddlecum to the prison, which was on the other side of the town. The sun rose as he crossed the Square, and the windows of the houses blinked in the morning light, and the bowl of the sky was like a Chinese tea-cup that you can almost see through, and a flock of little clouds stood perfectly still, like sheep when a strange dog first appears. Mr. Justice Rumple felt happier than he had been for a long time, and hurried to the prison as fast as he could. How delighted the poor Members of the Jury would be, he thought, when they heard that he had decided to release them! They would probably give him three cheers, he decided.

He pulled the big brass bell at the prison gate, and heard it ring far inside: *Inkle-bangle-bankle-bang. Inkle-bangle-bankle-bang. Inkle-bangle, inkle-bangle, bang.*

No one came to let him in, so he pulled it again and again: *Inkle-bangle, inkle-bangle, inkle-bangle-bankle-bang . . .*

Then a window opened, and another and another and another, and all the prisoners put out their heads and shouted, 'Who's making all that noise?'

'I am!' shouted the Judge. 'I've come to tell you that I've changed my mind, and you can all go home. You can go home at once!'

'I'm not going home at this time in the morning for you or anyone else!' shouted Mr. Whitloe the drayman, and shut his window with a bang.

'Aren't we even allowed to sleep?' yelled Mrs. Leathercow, and shut her window with a still louder bang.

'You don't think we're going before we've had breakfast, do you?' exclaimed Mr. Fullalove, and shut his window too.

'Go away!' shouted all the others. 'Wait till we've had our breakfast!' And they all shut their windows very firmly indeed.

An expression of great sadness settled on the Judge's face, but making an effort he decided to be patient, and sitting down on a grassy bank opposite the prison gate he lighted a cigar and prepared to wait until nine o'clock, which was the usual breakfast-time at Midmeddlecum Gaol.

Far above him, while he sat there smoking, a great bird crossed the sky, then turned in a wide sweep, circled above him, and presently flew swiftly to Major Palfrey's house, where he landed on a window-ledge and with his beak tapped loudly on the glass.

Dinah and Dorinda woke immediately and let the Falcon in.

'I think your plan has worked,' he said. 'The Judge is sitting outside the prison, waiting, I suppose, till the slugabeds wake and let him in.'

'He has changed his mind!' exclaimed Dinah.

'And Mr. Corvo will be free,' said Dorinda, clapping her hands.

'So it appears,' said the Falcon.

'We must go at once,' said Dinah, 'and take away the kippers and the mice and the eels before the Judge gets back. Hurry up and get dressed, Dorinda. Good-bye, Falcon, and thank you for coming. We'll see you very soon!'

So the Falcon flew away, and Dinah and Dorinda got dressed in three minutes, and ran all the way across the fields to the Judge's house.

Just before they reached it they saw the Cook and the Tablemaid and

76

the Housemaid hurrying in the direction of Midmeddlecum, for the news had spread rapidly, and everybody by now had heard what was happening, and practically all the inhabitants except very small babies and people who were bedridden were on their way to the prison to see the release of the Members of the Jury.

So Dinah and Dorinda found it quite easy to remove the mice from under the bed, and the kippers from the dining-room wall, and the eels from the Greek vase, and quickly they buried them in one of the Judge's own flower-beds. Then they washed their hands and ran to the prison too.

They were in plenty of time, for the Members of the Jury still refused to leave until they had had their breakfast, and would not even allow Mrs. Jehu to serve it half an hour before the usual time.

But at half-past nine they came out, looking very serious and important, and the Judge stood on a chair and politely announced that he had changed his mind, and so they would be released from prison and could go where they liked and do as they pleased—'Within reason, of course, always within reason,' he quickly added.

To think and talk about

A 1. Dorinda and Dinah 'both heartily disliked Catherine Crumb'. Why then did they ask for her help?

2. Do you think the judge knew the smells were real or did he really believe his imagination was playing tricks on him?

3. When the judge told the jury they could go home they made all sorts of excuses why they wouldn't go immediately. Why do you think they made these excuses?

4. When Judge Rumple changed his mind he felt 'happier than he had been for a long time'. There could be several reasons for this feeling. What do you think they were?

B 1. Which part of Dorinda and Dinah's plan do you think worked best?

2. What would you have added to Dorinda and Dinah's plan to make really sure it would work?

3. What do you think Mr Corvo has done to land in jail and make the judge so sure he is guilty?

4. What do you think would have happened if the judge had discovered the three smelly objects?

C 1. What would you have done if you were the judge?

2. With which part of the plan would you have liked to be involved?

3. As the story developed perhaps your feelings towards the judge changed. How did your feelings change?

4. Do you think the story 'Change Your Mind' is far fetched? Which parts of the story are the most difficult to believe?

More books to read

1. *Harriet the Spy* by Louise Fitzhugh
   Harriet's friends weren't too pleased to read the things she had written about them in her secret notebook. An amusing story which you're sure to enjoy.

2. *Mistress Masham's Repose* by T. H. White
   The story of how Maria is saved from her wicked guardian's evil plots with the help of the tiny people she finds living in the grounds of the huge old house in which she lives.

3. *Apple Bough* by Noel Streatfield
   If you've ever longed to be home then you'll understand why the Forum children were fed up travelling round the country following Sebastian who gave concerts on his violin.

To write about

What do you think would have happened if Dorinda and Dinah's plan had not worked?
Imagine you are one of the children of the town of Midmeddlecum.
Can you write a story of your part in Dorinda and Dinah's second plan to make Judge Justice Rumple 'Change his mind'?

You'd Better Believe Him
A Fable

Discovered an old rocking-horse in Woolworth's,
He tried to feed it but without much luck
So he stroked it, had a long conversation about
The trees it came from, the attics it had visited.
Tried to take it out then
But the store detective he
Called the police who in court the next morning said
'He acted strangely when arrested,
His statement read simply "I believe in rocking-
horses."
We have reason to believe him mad.'
'Quite so,' said the prosecution,
'Bring in the rocking horse as evidence.'
'I'm afraid it's escaped, sir,' said the store manager,
'Left a hoof print as evidence
On the skull of the store detective.'
'Quite so,' said the prosecution, fearful
of the neighing
Out in the corridor.

Brian Patten

Searching for missing words

In the passage some words have been missed out.
Can you be sure which words have been missed out?
Sometimes there can be only one answer.
Sometimes there can be several answers for you to think and
talk about.
How many words can you find?

Toby pulled his horse to a walking pace lest the wood should
be slippery, and expected that Feste would cross it as he had
done hundreds of time before. But no; Feste, the obedient,
_____ not cross it. He sidled and _____ but he would not go
on. Toby _____ to him, coaxed him, scolded him, _____ his
head round to face the _____ again and again, but all in
_____. At last, for the first time _____ his life he lifted his
_____ and lashed him. Feste reared up and _____ at the air
with outstretched fore-feet _____ that it was all Toby could
_____ to hang on in the saddle. _____ in this way Feste had
exhibited his _____ and his strength and his angry _____, he
came down from his prancing _____ without warning leapt
the high _____ at the side of the lane.

From *The Children of Green Knowe* by Lucy Boston

81

What's the truth?

Andrewbank School has a school newspaper.
Clare and Colin, the editors, wrote this description of their paper.

The Andrewbank Times keeps you up to date with all the news of the school and the town. Not only that, but we give careful comment on what's happening in our page one opinion column. The layout is striking and the headlines are eyecatching.

Our illustrations are all original but the editors demand a high standard especially on our front page. We have articles for everybody including sport, letters, school events, stories, and many others. We're sure you'll look forward each week to the Andrewbank Times with eager delight.

One of the less kind pupils named Tony wrote this to the letters page. Here are some of his comments:

What a disappointment! For a start there is no 'news' in the Andrewbank Times—it's all ancient history and very boring. The drawings are childish and often have nothing to do with the articles with which they appear.

It's clear the editors don't have two original ideas to rub together. Too many of the stories are about sport—does nothing else ever happen except soccer matches? I think the paper needs new blood particularly on the editorial staff. Unfortunately, I think I will be too busy this session, but I could help out now and then if I was asked. Andrewbank Times could be good, given guidance.

Talk about these two accounts.
How have Clare and Colin tried to give a good impression of the newspaper?
Can Tony's view of the paper be believed?

Going to the Library

Have you been to your local library?
Did you find out how the books are arranged?
In most libraries the books *other than the fiction*, that is all the information books or **non-fiction** are usually given a number which is marked on the spine. A man called Melvin Dewey invented this system of numbering library books, and it is called the **Dewey system**. Here it is:

There are nine hundred and ninety nine sections!

0 to 99	General books, encyclopaedias, dictionaries, etc
100 to 199	Books about the way we think about life
200 to 299	Books on different religions
300 to 399	Books on society, law and money
400 to 499	Languages of the world
500 to 599	Science
600 to 699	Engineering, farming, building, etc
700 to 799	The arts—music, painting, and sports
800 to 899	Literature, poetry, plays
900 to 999	History, geography and travel

Can you find out more about this system?
Is it used in your local library?
If not, what other system is used?

I Had a Hippopotamus

I had a hippopotamus; I kept him in a shed
And fed him upon vitamins and vegetable bread;
I made him my companion on many cheery walks,
And had his portrait done by a celebrity in chalks.

His charming eccentricities were known on every
    side,
The creature's popularity was wonderfully wide;
He frolicked with the Rector in a dozen friendly
    tussles,
Who could not but remark upon his
    hippopotamuscles.

If he should be afflicted by depression or the dumps,
By hippopotameasles or the hippopotamumps,
I never knew a particle of peace till it was plain
He was hippopotamasticating properly again.

I had a hippopotamus; I loved him as a friend;
But beautiful relationships are bound to have an end;
Time takes, alas! our joys from us and robs us of our
    blisses;
My hippopotamus turned out a hippopotamissis.

My housekeeper regarded him with jaundice in her
    eye;
She did not want a colony of hippopotami;
She borrowed a machine-gun from her soldier-
    nephew, Percy,
And showed my hippopotamus no hippopotamercy.

My house now lacks the glamour that the charming
    creature gave,
The garage where I kept him is as silent as the grave;
No longer he displays among the motor-tyres and
    spanners
His hippopotamastery of hippopotamanners.

No longer now he gambols in the orchards in the
    spring;
No longer do I lead him through the village on a
    string;
No longer in the mornings does the neighbourhood
    rejoice
To his hippopotamusically-modulated voice.

I had a hippopotamus; but nothing upon earth
Is constant in its happiness or lasting in its mirth;
No joy that life can give me can be strong enough
    to smother
My sorrow for that might-have-been-a-
    hippopotamother.

Patrick Barrington

Read and remember

Can you read carefully and remember what you've read?
Here is a short story. Read it carefully and try to remember the
events as they are told in the story.
Do you think you'll remember when you turn to page 91?

The Holiday

After such dreadful weather no one could have been more
delighted than Val to welcome this spell of warm sunshine. She
had suffered a long illness which had kept her indoors for
several months, and was longing to get out into the fresh air.

Val's parents could afford to take their daughter on a trip
almost anywhere in the world, but she wanted a simple holiday
in the peaceful seclusion of the countryside. There she could
wander at her leisure, exploring unspoilt beauty spots, and
eating good food.

It was with great excitement that the family had set off, taking
with them their pet spaniel, Rob. Soon their green estate car was
out of the traffic and moving along country lanes.

Right from the start all the family loved the quaint cottage
nestling amid the tangled greenery of the garden. Rob explored
at once and was soon very excited.

Unpacking was left until later. A meal was prepared in the
large kitchen and Val made her plans. She intended that the next
two weeks would be the best the family ever had.

And so they were. The weather helped, but really the beauty of
the countryside and the family's determination to enjoy
themselves made the difference. Val returned home happy, but
more importantly, restored to full health once again.

Now turn to page 91.

Reading for the main idea

Emma was working on a project about **rivers** and came across this passage in a book.

Of Europe's many rivers the Rhine is the most important, flowing on its course to the North Sea, through Switzerland, Germany, and the Netherlands. It acts as part of the boundaries between Switzerland and Austria, Switzerland and Germany, Germany and France, and many old fortified buildings still line its banks today. For the most part this river is deep, wide, and flows slowly making it ideal for trade purposes—many goods are transported by barge. Since the Rhine passes through so many countries, there is a great variety of farming carried on along its banks depending on the height of the land, the soil, and the climate. These include the rearing of cattle on high slopes, orchards and vineyards, and the growing of wheat, sugarbeet, hops, tobacco, and barley on the flatter, more fertile slopes.

Emma made notes of the main ideas of this passage. Here is part of the diagram she made. Can you add the other main ideas and use arrows to show supporting details?

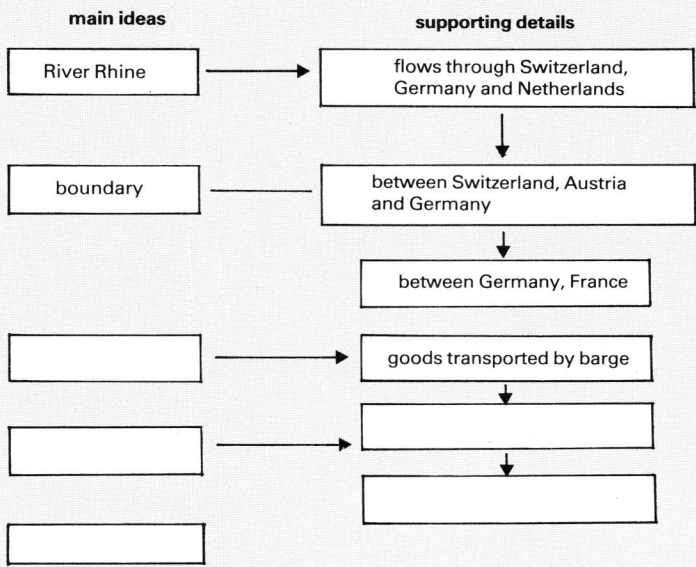

To talk and write about

1. Dorinda and Dinah 'both heartily disliked Catherine Crumb, with her wicked face and her long thin legs, and they had by no means forgiven her for what she had once done to them when, after eating too much, they had swollen into something like balloons.'
Do you think you could make up the story which ends with Dorinda and Dinah looking like balloons?

2. Have you ever been ignored like Justice Rumple?
Write your diary for a week in which you have fallen out with your friends.
Try to express how you would feel.
How do you win back your friends?

3. Look at the illustrations of Justice Rumple.
Talk about the kind of man he is.
Now write a clear description of Mr Justice Rumple.
Have sentences about his appearance and his manner.
Try to say what you think of him and whether you like him or not.

How on earth!

Talk about the strange scene in the picture.
How might it have happened?
Could you write a story about it?

To write about

What do you think of when you look at this picture?

Could you write about what you imagine has happened or is about to happen in this place?

Is it in the passage?

Carol wrote this article for her school newspaper.

Last week I went shopping for a new pair of jeans. My old pair were past their best since I had worn them every week for nearly a year. I wanted a pair in the same style.

Would you believe that I tried four likely shops with no luck? I was despairing when a shop assistant told me why I was having trouble. 'Sorry dear,' she said, 'your jeans are out of fashion.' Out of fashion after one year! I couldn't believe it.

But I had to. You see, they change the fashion every so often so that (they hope) people will throw away the old style and buy the new. And they do! People like to keep up with fashion but really I feel we are just being conned by the shops.

So look out for other examples, and be warned. Wear what you want to wear, not what they tell you is 'in fashion'.

Read the sentences below and then put them into three groups:
- (a) Facts which are in the passage
- (b) Opinions which are in the passage
- (c) Facts or opinions which are *not* in the passage.

1. Carol went shopping and found the shops in her town were no longer selling jeans.
2. It is unbelievable that jeans should go out of fashion after one year.
3. Carol went into four shops.
4. Carol was told by a shop assistant why she couldn't buy jeans in the style she wanted.
5. People simply throw old-style clothes away.
6. The fashion is changed frequently so that people keep buying new clothes.
7. If you keep up with fashion you are just being tricked into buying new clothes.
8. Carol decided to buy the new style jeans.
9. Many people like to keep up with fashion.
10. Everybody should wear just what he or she likes.

Act it out

Could you write a short play of the story, 'Change Your Mind'?
Include the scenes in the Judge's house, with the Judge, the
cook, the housemaid, and the others in his house taking part.
When you have written it, act the play for your friends.

Read and remember

Can you put the sentences below in the same order as in 'The
Holiday' on page 86?
Don't look back to the story.

(a) The family were excited as they set off and they were soon
     moving along country lanes.

(b) They left the unpacking until later and had a meal while
     making plans to have a great family holiday.

(c) Val was delighted to see the sun and since she had been ill
     she longed to go out in the air.

(d) The holiday was the best they had ever had because
     everyone was determined to enjoy themselves, especially
     Val who returned home in good health.

(e) Val wanted a simple holiday in the country even although
     her parents could have taken her anywhere in the world.

(f) At once her family loved the cottage and the scenery and
     Rob explored right away.

The company words keep

These two pictures are of the same beach, at different times of year.
Joe wrote the following about the first picture.

> It was the hottest day of the summer. The donkeys were hard worked by the unending queue of excited children, and Vernon Manson's Punch and Judy Show was surrounded by a crowd of eager-faced youngsters, laughter in their eyes.

Can you continue Joe's description of the summer beach scene?

The second picture shows the beach very differently.
Here is how Joe started to describe it.

> It was a sad scene. The deserted stalls along the front might
> have been crying, for they were running with the salty tears
> which the wind whipped up from the sea.

Try to finish the description of the second picture.

Following Instructions

How to Make Lemonade

Cooking time 5 minutes

2 large lemons
1-2 tablespoons sugar
1 litre boiling water

Cut the lemons in half. Squeeze the juice from the lemons into a jug. Put the squeezed halves, sugar and boiling water into a second jug. Allow to cool, pressing the lemon halves to extract the maximum flavour. Strain into a jug with the lemon juice. If wished, the lemon peel and sugar may be boiled with the water for 5 minutes. Then strain the lemonade into the jug.
Serves 4.

Orangeade

Use 2 large oranges, or 2 medium oranges and a lemon, and continue as above.
Note: The juice of the fruit should never be heated, as this would destroy the vitamin C content.

Talk about the recipe for lemonade.
Could you follow it?
Do you know what vitamin C is?
Why not try making lemonade in your class or at home?
Can you write out a recipe for making orangeade?

The way words are built

New words are coming into our language all the time.
One way in which we get new words is by borrowing them from other languages. Often, if something new comes from another country, we get not only the new thing, but its name from the language of that country. For instance, when a new breed of dog was brought from Germany about a hundred years ago, we found a new word in our language. It was the name of the dog—the *Dachshund*.

Below are pairs of words which English has borrowed from other languages.

Both words in each pair came from the same language. The languages from which the words came are in the box on the right, but they are not in the correct order.
Can you match the words to the languages?

1 judo   origami

2 cafe   discotheque

3 macaroni   violin

4 budgerigar   kangaroo

5 trek   commando

6 bungalow   jungle

7 syrup   giraffe

8 ketchup   tea

9 stampede   guitar

10 marzipan   snorkel

German

Chinese

Hindi (one of the languages of India)

Australian Aboriginal (spoken by natives of Australia)

French

Japanese

Italian

Afrikaans (spoken by some of the white people in South Africa, it is like Dutch)

Arabic

Spanish

If you do not know the right answers can you think of a way of finding out where the words came from?

Thomas Kempe lived in the sixteenth century. His ghost now haunts the house and town in which James Harrison lives. Thomas Kempe writes notes to James telling him what he wants. As this story shows, Thomas Kempe also has ways of showing who he doesn't like. Poor James doesn't know what to do about Thomas Kempe. As the story begins he had just failed to convince his friend Simon that Thomas Kempe really exists. Things get worse when the vicar comes to tea.

This extract is taken from a book called *The Ghost of Thomas Kempe* by Penelope Lively.

The Ghost of Thomas Kempe

Simon vanished, leaving James with feelings of resentment: there was no doubt about it, Simon was only half-involved in the problem of Thomas Kempe. Interested, prepared to help up to a point, but not, like James, plunged into it day and night, like it or not.

He was still facing this fact, which made him feel isolated but, at the same time, challenged, like heroes of old confronted with impossibly difficult tasks, when he reached Mrs Verity's cottage. Mrs Verity was sitting on a chair in the doorway, enjoying the afternoon sunshine and keeping an eye on the various activities of East End Lane.

'Who'd like a mint humbug?'

'Yes, please,' said James.

'Let's see now, they were in my pinny pocket . . . Here we are, dear. I've just seen your mother go past with her shopping so she'll be back now. There was one of those Bakery bags in her basket so I expect she's got something nice for your tea. There's nurse's car—I wonder where she's going?' Mrs Verity shifted her chair slightly to improve her view of the street. 'The telly repair van's still outside the Bradley's, I see. That's the best part of an hour he's been there.'

James stared up at Mrs Verity's thatched roof, admiring the patterned bit at the top and thinking that it must be very dull just being interested in what other people were up to. Starlings sat on the ridge of the roof, whistling and chattering. They gave the impression of doing much the same as Mrs Verity.

Mrs Verity was talking about school. She asked James how he liked it and James said it was all right thanks and told her a bit about the project they were doing and Mrs Verity said 'Fancy!' and 'Dear me, it wasn't like that in my day.' And then rather surprisingly, she began to tell James a long story about a Sunday School when she was a small girl that began most unpromisingly and suddenly got very funny and unexpected. The Sunday School, it seemed, was a weekly session of torment during which all the Ledsham children of the time were made to sit in the cold and dusty silence of the church hall for two hours on end listening to the Scriptures read aloud, neither moving nor speaking on pain of instant and dreadful punishment. And on one never-to-be-forgotten occasion the children had slowly and delightedly become aware that the Vicar's dour sister who was responsible for inflicting this torture upon them was herself falling inexorably asleep . . .

'We all looked at each other and nobody hardly dared breathe and we waited till she dozed right off, sitting there in her chair with the Bible in her hand, and then my brother Robert—he was ever such a wicked boy, my brother, always in hot water, but he did well for himself later, manager of the Co-op in Rugby he was till he retired—Robert signed to us all and we all got up, quiet as mice—not a sound, and we crept out and left her there and we turned the key in the lock behind us. And then we rushed out into the sunshine whooping and screeching like a lot of little savages and we played a wild game in the churchyard, in and out the gravestones. I can remember it now. Though it seems funny to think back—you hardly feel it could be the same person as you are now. But they say the child is father to the man, don't they?' She looked anxiously at James as though wondering whose father he might be and James stared back at her with a new interest. Somewhere, deep within stout, elderly Mrs Verity, with her rheumaticky hands that swelled up around her wedding ring, and her bad back that bothered her in damp weather, there sheltered the memory of a little girl who had behaved outrageously in Sunday School. And that, when you stopped to think about it, was a very weird thing indeed.

He was just about to ask what happened when the Vicar's sister woke up when a tremendous gust of wind sent the starlings tumbling off the roofs—Mrs Verity's dress ballooned around her.

'Gracious! What a gale! I'll have to go inside.'

Air formed itself into a solid pressure on James' right arm, tugging him away from Mrs Verity's door. Another bank of it hustled him down the lane towards East End Cottage. Mrs Verity was controlling her skirts with one hand and pulling her chair into the house with the other.

'Goodbye for now, dear.'

James shouted 'Goodbye' as the wind gave him a final shove on to the opposite pavement and instantly subsided. Seething with indignation he ran the rest of the way home.

Bully. Busybody. Who does he think he is? I can talk to Mrs Verity if I want to, can't I?'

Does he think he owns me, or something?

Mrs Verity had been right about the Bakery bag. There were cream splits for tea, which James found very heartening. After a while he felt sufficiently restored to tease Helen about her new dress.

'What's it s'posed to be? I never saw such a weird object. Oh, I know—it's a football jersey that someone left out in the rain so it got all soggy and stretched so it wasn't any use any more . . .'

'It's a striped shift. Julia's got one too.'

'It's shifted all right. Shifted in all the wrong directions. Why's it such a peculiar shape—oh, *sorry*, that's you, I thought it was the dress . . .'

'Mum!' wailed Helen.

'Enough!' said Mrs Harrison. 'And finish your tea, please. I want to clear up before the Vicar comes.'

'The *Vicar*?'

'About the choir.'

The Vicar, however, arrived before Mrs Harrison had had time to establish order in the kitchen. Moreover, he was one of those people who like to make it instantly clear that they are unusually easy going, and refused to be steered into the sitting-room.

'Please—I do hate people to put themselves out—just carry on as though I weren't here.'

That, thought James, would be a bit difficult. The Vicar was six feet tall and stout into the bargain. He had already clipped his head on a beam as he came in and was trying desperately to suppress a grimace of pain.

'Oh dear,' said Mrs Harrison, sweeping crockery into the sink. 'These blessed ceilings. I'm so sorry. Will you have a cup of tea? I'll just make some fresh.'

The front door slammed with a loud bang, making the Vicar jump. 'I never refuse a cup of tea—but please—I don't want to be a nuisance.'

'No trouble,' said Mrs Harrison. 'James, do something about that dog. It seems to have gone mad.'

Tim had gone into the now familiar routine that indicated, James realized with a sinking heart, that Thomas Kempe was not far away. He grabbed him. The Vicar, too, was looking at him, though apparently for different reasons.

'Dear me, how like the stray who got in and took the joint from our larder last week. Curious to see two mongrels so much alike, eh? Well, well. And how's school, young man?'

'Fine,' said James, 'thanks.' Tim was struggling violently, and lunging with bared teeth at a point somewhere behind the Vicar. The windows rattled. 'These autumn winds,' said the Vicar. 'I always think of those at sea.'

'What?' said Mrs Harrison. 'Oh, yes, yes, quite.' She slammed the lid on the teapot irritably.

The electric light flickered. Upstairs, distantly, came the sound of an alarm clock going off. A cup jinked in its saucer on the dresser.

'Do sit down,' said Mrs Harrison. 'James, pull up a chair for the Vicar.'

James fetched the windsor chair from the corner and placed it by the table. He still had one hand on its arm as the Vicar began to lower himself into it, and so felt the whole thing twitch, stagger, and jerk suddenly sideways, so that the Vicar, prodded violently in the hip, lurched against the table and almost fell.

'James!' said Mrs Harrison angrily. 'Look what you're doing!'

'Sorry,' said James in confusion, straightening the chair. The Vicar sat down, rubbing his hip and also apologizing. Tim began to bark hysterically.

'Put that dog out!' shouted Mrs Harrison.

With Tim outside, things were quieter, except for another bang as the back door, this time, slammed. The Vicar passed a hand across his forehead and rubbed his head, furtively.

'Family life, eh! There's always something going on, what?'

'Never a dull moment,' said Mrs Harrison grimly. 'Milk?'

'Oh—please—yes, if I may . . . So kind of you. I do hope I'm not interrupting. I'm sure you're very busy, like we all are these days, eh?'

'Not at all,' said Mrs Harrison. 'James, pass the Vicar his tea, will you?'

James, with extreme caution, carried cup and saucer across the room. He was standing in front of the Vicar, and the Vicar's fingers were just

closing on the edge of the saucer, when the cup jolted, tipped, hung at an angle of forty-five degrees, and turned over. Tea flowed into the saucer, and thence in a cascade on to the Vicar's trousers.

'James!' said Mrs Harrison in a strangled voice.

There was a great deal of mopping and exclaiming. The Vicar apologized, and then apologized again. James apologized. Mrs Harrison's face had taken on that pinched, gathered look that foretold an outburst as soon as circumstances permitted. Finally, the Vicar, dried off and supplied with a new cup of tea, stopped saying how sorry he was and began to talk about choir practices. Mrs Harrison liked to sing sometimes: she said it allowed her to let off steam. Furthermore, she thought it would be a good idea if James sang. James, knowing this, had been hoping to beat a retreat. He sidled towards the door. 'My son,' said Mrs Harrison, glaring at him, 'sings too. After a fashion.'

'My dear boy,' said the Vicar, 'you must come along. We've got some other chaps about your age.'

James mumbled that he'd love to, or words to that effect. He was pinned to the spot now, by a steely look from his mother.

'Splendid, eh?' said the Vicar. 'Tell you what, I'll just jot down the times of our practices, shall I?' He patted his pockets.

Mrs Harrison said, 'James. Fetch the telephone pad, please, and a pencil.'

James opened the kitchen door, which swung shut again behind him, and crossed the hall. The telephone pad had a shopping list on it which said 'Onions, cereals, elastic bands, disinfectant.' Underneath that was a message about an electrician who would call back later, and a picture of a spaceman (drawn by James), and underneath that was a message from Thomas Kempe in large letters, which said 'I am watchynge ye.'

'Go on and watch then,' shouted James, in a fury. 'See if I care!'

There was a crash. The barometer had leapt off the wall and lay on the floor, the glass cracked. And a series of loud bangs, apparently made by some kind of blunt instrument, such as a hammer, reverberated through the house.

The kitchen door flew open. The banging ceased instantly. Mrs. Harrison was standing there saying the kind of things that were to be expected, only slightly toned down in deference to the Vicar, who was standing behind her, with a dazed expression on his face. He had hit his head on the beam again, James realized.

'. . . must apologize for my son's appalling behaviour,' concluded Mrs Harrison.

'Boys will be boys,' said the Vicar, without conviction. 'Eh? And now I really must be on my way. So kind . . . So glad we can look forward to having you with us . . . Do hope I haven't kept you from anything . . .' He edged sideways through the front door, stooping, with the air of a man who wanted only to be unobtrusive and had always wished himself several sizes smaller.

James picked up the barometer and waited for the wrath to come.

Upstairs, later, James catalogued the extent of his mother's displeasure in the Personal Notebook. 'No pudding, obviously. Maybe I'll die of starvation, and *then* they'll be sorry. Bed straight after supper. Which is why I'm here. No Simon to play for two days.'

He turned over the page, and a new message confronted him, written with surly disregard across a whole clean page of the notebook.

I lyke not Priestes.

James tore it out, screwed it into a ball, and hurled it across the room.

To think and talk about

A 1. Why do you think Mrs Verity is so interested in what other people are doing?

2. What problems does Thomas Kempe cause James?

3. What would Mrs Harrison say if she were told that all the disasters were the fault of Thomas Kempe?

4. Why does James think it is a very weird thing that in Mrs Verity 'there sheltered the memory of a little girl who had behaved outrageously in Sunday School'?

5. Do you think the vicar would ever complain about anything? Give some reasons for your answer.

B 1. How do you think James will get rid of Thomas Kempe?

2. Thomas Kempe doesn't like Mrs Verity or the vicar. What other people do you think he would dislike and what do you imagine he would do to them?

3. In Mrs Verity's account of childhood mischief what do you imagine did happen when the vicar's sister eventually woke up?

4. What orders do you think Thomas Kempe will give James?

C 1. What would you have done to convince people that Thomas Kempe existed?

2. If *you* were the ghost what havoc would you create?

3. What do you think of the way James treats his sister Helen? Is this anything to do with Thomas Kempe?

4. What do you think of this story? Were you frightened or amused? Give some reasons why you liked or disliked the story.

More books to read

1. *The Ghost Downstairs* by Leon Garfield
   In return for riches Mr Fast agrees to give seven years off the
   end of his life to Mr Fishbane. This story should make you
   think, and not just about ghosts.

2. *The Ghost's Companion* by Peter Haining
   Exciting ghost stories. You're sure to find one to give you a
   scare!

3. *A Wrinkle in Time* by Madelaine L'Engle
   A search for a lost father through a wrinkle in time leads
   Charles Wallace Murray to a planet where a huge evil brain
   known as IT is in command.

Spot the howler

Alastair was tuning his violin with a frowning face.

Searching for missing words

In the passage some words have been missed out.
Can you be sure which words have been missed out?
Sometimes there can only be one answer.
Sometimes there can be several answers for you to think and talk about.
How many words can you find?

So Septimus stood, aware of the one sound which was the thumping of his own heart. The seconds crawled by and grew into minutes and still Septimus stood, motionless as the invisible pillars of the crypt. Then, at last, his _____ was rewarded. There was a swift _____ of movement in the blackness. It _____ cut off as suddenly as it _____. It was not a mouse or a _____. A human being had moved somewhere _____ the blackness of the crypt. Septimus _____ the torch, trying to gauge the _____ of the sound. The beam stabbed _____ in the blackness illuminating a dark _____ of pillars and arches. They seemed _____ white in the sudden light and _____ threw a herring bone of black _____. In the very edge of the _____ there was a flicker of movement. _____ swung the torch, and momentarily there was the _____ of a man.

From *Septimus and the Minster Ghost* by Stephen Chance

To write about

Imagine you are in James's place.
Write about the further trouble Thomas Kempe gets you into.
How do you manage to rid yourself of Thomas Kempe?

What's the truth?

Stephen went to a pop concert one evening and wrote a report
for the school newspaper.
Here is what he wrote.

The dreadful din began as soon as the group took to the stage.
After ten minutes the thumping beat had caused widespread
headaches. The weird electronic sounds didn't make any sense
while the group who claimed to be entertainers pranced around
the stage. The moaning noises, I'm told, were the lyrics of a
song, not that any of the words could be understood. Some
hysterical teenagers seemed to enjoy the evening although they
appeared to have dressed at a rather poor jumble sale before
coming. All in all it was a ghastly experience and I'm amazed
they didn't pay people to come and listen.

Tina also was there and wrote this report for the paper.

As soon as the enthusiastic fans gathered it was clear we were in
for something special. And so it proved to be. The group was
nothing short of brilliant, showing tremendous skill in creating a
completely new sound. Not only was the music exciting but the
group was able to convey a real message through the words of
the songs which is unusual these days. What we witnessed is the
beginning of a new direction for the pop world. This has been
long overdue and it's fortunate we have such a group around to
revive the pop scene.

Sandra, the editor of the newspaper had a difficult job deciding
which report to use.
Talk about the ways in which Stephen and Tina have used words
and statements to support their view of the concert.

Posting Letters

There are no lamps in our village,
And when the owl-and-bat black night
Creeps up low fields
And sidles along the manor walls
I walk quickly.

It is winter;
The letters patter from my hand
Into the tin box in the cottage wall;
The gate taps behind me,
And the road in the sliver of moonlight
Gleams greasily
Where the tractors have stood.

I have to go under the spread fingers of the trees
Under the dark windows of the old man's house,
Where the panes in peeling frames
Flash like spectacles
As I tip-toe.
But there is no sound of him in his one room
In the Queen Anne shell,
Behind the shutters.

I run past the gates,
Their iron feet gaitered with grass,
Into the church porch,
Perhaps for sanctuary,
Standing, hand on the cold door ring,
While above
The tongue-tip of the clock
Clops
Against the hard palate of the tower.

The door groans as I push
And
Dare myself to dash
Along the flagstones to the great brass bird,
To put one shrinking hand
Upon the gritty lid
Of Black Tom's tomb.

Don't tempt whatever spirits stir
In this damp corner,
But
Race down the aisle,
Blunder past font,
Fumble the door,
Leap steps,
Clang iron gate,
And patter through the short-cut muddy lane.

Oh, what a pumping of breath
And choking throat
For three letters.
And now there are the cattle
Stirring in the straw
So close
I can hear their soft muzzling and coughs;
And there are the bungalows,
And the steel-blue miming of the little screen;
And the familiar rattle of the latch,
And our own knocker
Clicking like an old friend;
And
I am home.

Gregory Harrison

Read and remember

Can you read carefully and remember what you've read?
Here is a short story. Read it carefully and try to remember the events as they are told in the story.
Do you think you'll remember when you turn to page 114?

Disturbance at Night

The evening air was suddenly disturbed by the crack of gunshots. The campers were immediately awake and emerged from the tents to investigate. As further shots rang out, the youngsters became aware of the thump-thumping of some wild animal running for its life. It was coming crashing through the trees and must be a fairly large deer.

Sure enough, within a minute the terrified beast came charging into the clearing and rushed straight past. One tent was knocked over and the youngsters had to dive for cover. More noises followed, this time accompanied by shouts and curses. Jane shone her torch in the direction of the pursuers. Bill shouted as loudly and as gruffly as he could.

The effect was immediate. The deer poachers turned at the sight of light and the sound of a voice. Their panic and desperation to get clear were obvious. Bill continued to shout and was joined by the others.

Later the young people congratulated themselves on saving the deer from its enemy. They also had a good laugh to think that the poachers were tricked so easily.

Now turn to page 114.

To talk and write about

Imagine you are convinced you have seen a ghost. You decide to tell the local police constable. Write the conversation you have with the policeman.

Perhaps your conversation might begin like this:

P.C: 'Well, youngster, what can we do for you?'
You: 'I've definitely seen a ghost by the old castle. I think you'd better come and have a look.'
P.C: 'A ghost, eh? With or without a head?'
You: 'I don't think you believe me . . .'
P.C: 'Now what makes you think that? Tell me, did your ghost rattle his chains and make the usual ghost noises?'

Make up the rest of the conversation.

The Man who Wasn't There

Yesterday upon the stair
I met a man who wasn't there;
He wasn't there again today,
I wish, I wish, he'd go away.

I've seen his shapeless shadow-coat
Beneath the stairway, hanging about;
And outside, muffled in a cloak
The same colour as the dark;

I've seen him in a black, black suit
Shaking, under the broken light;
I've seen him swim across the floor
And disappear beneath the door;

And once, I almost heard his breath
Behind me, running up the path:
Inside, he leant against the wall,
And turned . . . and was no one at all.

Yesterday upon the stair
I met a man who wasn't there;
He wasn't there again today,
I wish, I wish, he'd go away.

Brian Lee

Writing Letters

One day Victor was out on his bike and was freewheeling downhill when he hit a large pothole in the road and fell off. Although he was not injured himself, Vic's bike had a badly buckled front wheel, and it cost a lot to repair. He decided to write to the county roads department to complain about the state of the road he had been cycling on.

Here is the letter Vic wrote (with help from his Dad).

```
The Roads Manager,                       20 Thrush Street,
Menville District Council,               Menville
Town Hall,
Menville
                                         10th June


Dear Sir,

On the morning of 8th June I was cycling down Bunn's
Hill, when my bicycle hit a large hole in the road.  I
was unhurt, although I was thrown off my bicycle.  The
bicycle needed extensive repairs.  I enclose the receipt
for these from the bicycle shop.  As I feel that the
accident was caused by the state of the road, I am
writing to ask you to consider paying for the repairs.

Yours faithfully,


Victor Price

Victor Price
```

There are many official people you might need to write to at one time or another. Imagine that you have been travelling on a bus, and have left something in it. Write the letter you might send to the bus company about it. Talk about who you would write to, and the details you would give in your letter.

Read and remember

Can you put the sentences below in the same order as in the story 'Disturbances at Night' on page 110?
Don't look back to the story.

(a) A tent was knocked over as the terrified beast charged past.

(b) At the sight of light and the sound of voices the poachers at once ran away.

(c) Gunshots rang out and wakened the campers.

(d) More noises followed and Jane shone her torch while Bill shouted.

(e) More shots rang out and the noise of a wild animals was clearly heard.

(f) Later the youngsters were pleased they had been able to help save the deer from the poachers.

Act it out

Thomas Kempe does not seem to have been a very frightening ghost.
But some are.
With two friends, talk about the following scene.
The three of you are in a haunted house.
You have accepted a dare to stay there for the night of the full moon.
What will happen?
Act the scene.

Using a dictionary

1. Look up each word in bold type below in your dictionary. Which meaning from the dictionary is used in each sentence?

   fuse
   (a) What a time for the lights to **fuse**!
   (b) The heat was enough to make the strands of wire **fuse** together.
   (c) They moved back quickly, as the bomb had a very short **fuse**.

   force
   (a) The ship was sunk in a **force** 10 gale off Cape Wrath.
   (b) The burglar took out his tools and started to **force** the lock to the strongroom.
   (c) Jenny decided that she wanted to join the police **force** when she grew up.

   interest
   (a) What aroused my **interest** in gliding was the army camp nearby, where the recruits flew gliders at the weekends.
   (b) The rate of **interest** at the bank is high at present, so you would be ill-advised to borrow there.
   (c) Hudson makes a lot of money from the **interest** he has in a small airline.

2. Which of the three words in brackets is the best one to fit the sentence? If you can answer these without using a *large* dictionary you may well be a genius!

   (a) It was a (**magnanimous, malevolent, manifest**) gesture on the part of the theatre to give us free tickets for the children.
   (b) The price is (**eradicable, nominal, negotiable**) and I think we might be able to reduce it.
   (c) Despite the (**unreliability, precariousness, dubiety**) of the roadway, the convoy got through safely to the stranded villagers.
   (d) David could not make up his mind, but after ten minutes (**vacillation, oscillation, undulation**) he eventually chose the red jersey.

Here is a poem called

Time

What do we mean when we talk of time?
For time is a changing thing
We've lunch time and dinner time,
Summer, winter, play and work time.
Time can fly;
Weigh heavy on your hands.
Some have no time.
While there's a right time and a wrong time.
Sometime in the meantime.
And once upon a time-time.
Time can run out
Whether it be day time or night time.
And how do we spend our time?
Marking time or taking time
Or simply wasting time!

Now write your own poem about your favourite time.

The way words are built

Malapropisms

Mrs Malaprop was a funny character in a play written a long time ago. She keeps saying words which are *almost* right, but aren't. Here are some examples of the sort of thing she might have said.

1. John knows a lot about other countries. He is really good at geometry.

2. Dad played the fruit machine for a long time. Then he hit the jackboot.

3. Frank opened the kit and read the destructions very carefully.

4. Petra received a hard knock on the head and suffered from conclusion.

5. My Granny suffers badly from very close veins.

Mistakes of this kind are called malapropisms. Can you make up some malapropisms?

UNIT 35

Amanda and David are trying to help their Greek friend Yani who owes a large amount of money to the unpopular mayor of the town. They plan to kidnap all the donkeys on the island and blackmail the mayor into cancelling the debt. The children, however, have one or two problems to solve before they make their attempt at kidnapping the donkeys.

This story is taken from a book called *The Donkey Rustlers* by Gerald Durrell.

Sabotage!

'The first thing,' said Amanda, 'is to find out how many donkeys there are in the village. Do you know how many there are, Yani?'

Yani shrugged.

'I'm not sure,' he said. 'I've never counted them. Maybe twenty.'

'Well, we've got to be absolutely certain,' said Amanda, 'because there's no sense in our only taking half of them.'

'I still don't see how you are going to work this,' David said doubtfully.

'Shut up and listen,' said Amanda. 'As soon as we have found out how many donkeys there are, we then organise a gigantic raid so that we can get them all at once.'

'I think you're mad,' said David with conviction.

'Look, if we take them one at a time,' said Amanda, 'by the time we've taken three or four, the rest of the villagers will have become worried and put their donkeys under lock and key. We have to get them all at once, or else it's useless.'

'I still don't see how we can get twenty donkeys all at once,' said David, 'and then, when you've got them, what are you going to do with them?'

'Put them up in the hills somewhere,' said Amanda airily.

'I don't think that's a very good idea,' said Yani, 'because there's practically nowhere around here where you could hide twenty donkeys without somebody finding them. It would have to be a place which nobody would think of.'

'I know,' said Amanda, her eyes shining, 'we'll bring them out here.'

'What, to Hesperides?' asked David. 'I really think you *have* gone mad. How could we get them out here?'

'Well, how do *we* get out here?' said Amanda. 'We swim.'

'Yes, but *can* donkeys swim?' asked David.

Both children looked expectantly at Yani; Yani shrugged.

'I don't know,' he said. 'I've never thought about it. We don't use them for swimming. But certainly, if we hid the donkeys here, nobody would ever dream of looking for them on this island. That is a very good idea.'

'I think it's an absolutely harebrained scheme from beginning to end,' said David.

'Why don't you try it?' said Amanda.

David turned the idea over in his mind. The more he thought about the scheme the more pitfalls it seemed to possess, and the thought of his father's wrath if they were caught made him feel slightly sick. But, try as he would, he could not think of any alternative to Amanda's idea.

'All right,' he said reluctantly. 'But on one condition, that you leave the organising side of things to me and don't go doing anything stupid. It will have to be conducted like a military operation and the first thing to do is to find out how many donkeys there are in the village. The second thing to do is to find out whether donkeys can swim, because, if they can't swim, the whole scheme is useless.'

'Well, horses swim,' Amanda pointed out.

'I know. But it doesn't necessarily follow that donkeys can,' said David. 'Now, we must each have our own job to do so that we can spread out. First of all you and Yani and Coocos, if you can get hold of him, will go round the village and count the donkeys. While you are doing that I will work out a plan so that we can discover whether they can swim or not.'

'Why can't we just take one down to the beach and push him into the sea?' asked Amanda.

'You can't do that,' said David, 'because if somebody saw us it would give the whole game away. I'll think up something. Let's swim back now and you and Yani and Coocos can start counting.'

Excitedly the children swam back to the shore and climbed up the hillside towards the village.

Now that he had accepted Amanda's basic idea, David was really getting quite intrigued by the whole thing. It was, he confessed to himself, infinitely more interesting to organise this than to work out complicated sums about lizards and carts. So for the rest of the day David thought and thought of a way of finding out whether donkeys could swim, while Amanda, Yani and Coocos, armed with a pad and

120

pencil, solemnly went round the village making a list of people's donkeys; the interest with which they inquired after everybody's beasts of burden quite touched the villagers.

'It's a good thing,' said Yani, when they had almost completed their task, 'none of the donkeys have babies, for I think it would be very troublesome to get the baby ones over to the island.'

'Bah!' said Amanda, dismissing that with an airy wave of her hand, 'you could always row them over in a boat.'

By the time they had finished, the children had discovered that the village contained eighteen donkeys and one small horse. Five of the donkeys and the horse—they were delighted to discover—belonged to Mayor Oizus.

'Jolly well serve him right when we pinch his,' said Amanda. 'I bet that'll make him sweat even more than he sweats now.'

At firefly time the children held another council of war down in the olive groves. Amanda reported to David the number of donkeys and also, what was more important, where each one was stabled overnight.

'It's going to be a bit difficult,' said David gravely, studying the list. 'I think we could probably get away with nine or ten of them in one night, but how we are going to manage the rest I am not quite sure.'

'Well, next to Mayor Oizus,' said Amanda, 'the one who has the most is Papa Nikos.'

'And he always gets up very, very early and goes down to the fields,' said Yani. 'We might stand a chance of getting them there.'

'Anyway,' said Amanda impatiently, 'have you thought out how we can find out whether they can swim?'

'Yes,' admitted David, with a certain amount of smugness. 'I have thought up a very good idea. You know that river just before you get to the fields, with the little wooden bridge?'

'Yes,' said Amanda.

'Well, if we could sabotage that in some way so that when they lead a donkey across it it would collapse, we would find out whether the donkey could swim and, at the same time, it is not so deep that we couldn't rescue it if it *couldn't* swim.'

'David, that *is* a clever idea,' said Amanda, her eyes sparkling.

'But, how are you going to sabotage the bridge?' inquired Yani.

'Well, I went down and inspected it this afternoon,' said David. 'Actually it is so rickety that it doesn't require very much at all. I think if you just saw through the two centre supports, anything getting into the middle of it will push the whole thing into the water.'

Amanda gave a delighted crow of laughter.

'You are clever, David,' she said admiringly. 'I can't wait to do this. When shall we do it?'

'Well, the sooner the better,' said David. 'I thought we'd go down to-night, as there's no moon, and do it then. Then we can get up very early in the morning and go down there and watch. The trouble is we don't seem to have a saw in the house.'

'I've got a saw,' said Yani excitedly. 'I'll bring that.'

'Now remember, Coocos,' said David, pointing his finger sternly at the bowler-hatted boy, 'you are not to say a word to anybody about this.'

Coocos shook his head vigorously and crossed himself.

'No, Coocos won't say anything,' said Yani, 'because he's my friend.'

That night the children slipped quietly out of their bedrooms and down the stairs. Each creak made them start nervously for fear it would wake the General and bring his wrath down upon them. They finally got out of the house without disturbing their parents and made their way, together with Yani and Coocos, taking infinite and quite unnecessary precautions against being seen, to the little bridge that spanned the rather muddy canal on the edge of the corn fields. David stripped off his clothes and slipped into the brown water and disappeared under the bridge, having posted the rest of them at strategic points so that should the sound of sawing be heard by anyone who might come to investigate, they could all warn him. Then he set to work. In a very short time—for he found the wood was soft and semi-rotten—he succeeded in sawing through the two uprights that supported the centre of the bridge. He then uprooted them and replanted them in the mud so that, at a casual glance, they looked as if they were still supporting the bridge although in actual fact they were useless. He then climbed out on to the bank, carefully washing the mud from his legs, dressed himself, and then the children made their way back to their respective homes.

The sky was pearly pink and green with dawn light and there were still a few freckles of stars in it when David went into Amanda's room and woke her up. They went and met Yani and Coocos and made their way down in the fresh morning air to the little bridge. Conveniently close to the bridge several large clumps of bamboo were growing, which offered extremely good hiding places from which they could watch the result of their experiment and here they settled down and waited in silence for the first of the villagers to put in an appearance.

It was perhaps unfortunate that the first person to come down to the bridge that morning was Mayor Oizus himself. He was certainly the last

person the children had expected, for normally Mayor Oizus spent most of his time sitting in the local café, while Mrs Oizus did all the work in the fields, but the previous day Mrs Oizus had complained about some curious animal which seemed to be ruining the corn crop and so the Mayor had decided to take the unprecedented step of going down to see for himself. In order to save himself the arduous task of walking, he had decided to ride on one of his donkeys.

'Saint Polycarpos!' whispered Yani, his eyes wide. 'It's the Mayor himself.'

'Splendid,' said Amanda, starting to giggle.

'Shut up,' hissed David. 'He'll hear us.'

'He's going to be terribly angry,' said Yani.

'Serves him right,' said Amanda. 'That's what my father would call "poetic justice".'

They watched as the donkey, with great patience, considering the weight of the Mayor, plodded down the hillside and clip-clopped its way towards the bridge. It was very early and the Mayor, who was unaccustomed to such physical exertion as donkey-riding at dawn, was nodding sleepily as his mount jogged along. It came to the bridge and the children held their breath. It clattered on to the bridge and David watched in an agony of suspense, for he was not at all sure that his sabotage would work, but, to his intense delight, as the donkey reached the centre of the bridge, the whole thing gave way with a most satisfying scrunch, and both donkey and Mayor were precipitated into the water with a most glorious fountain-like splash, accompanied by a very heart-warming yell of fear from the Mayor.

'It worked!' said David, his eyes shining with excitement. 'It worked!'

'Absolutely wonderful!' Amanda exclaimed ecstatically.

'You did that very well, David,' said Yani.

However, they now discovered two things: that the donkey could swim remarkably well, and soon had itself out of the canal, whereas the Major could not swim at all.

'What shall we do?' said Yani. 'We can't let him drown. We'd better go and help him.'

The Mayor was clinging to a piece of driftwood from the bridge and bellowing for help at the top of his lungs, although at that hour in the morning it was unlikely, he felt, that there would be anybody around. He invoked the saints several times and tried to cross himself, but if he crossed himself he found he had to let go of the piece of wood, which was the only thing between himself and a watery grave.

'Yani can't go and help him,' said Amanda, 'because if he sees Yani he'll know, so we'd better go.'

Amanda and David ran along the bank towards the floundering Mayor.

'Don't worry, Mr Mayor,' shouted Amanda. 'We're coming.'

'Save me! Save me!' yelled the Mayor.

'Stop shouting, we're coming,' said David impatiently.

They made their way down the banks of the canal and plunged into the water.

'I'm drowning,' cried the Mayor in such a plaintive tone of voice that Amanda was seized with a fit of giggles.

'Be quiet,' said David soothingly. 'You are all right.'

The children got on each side of the portly Mayor and, supporting him under his armpits, they dragged him, dripping and covered with mud and water-weed, to the bank up which he scrambled looking not unlike a rather ungainly walrus getting out on to an ice floe. He presented a sight so comic that Amanda had to go and stand behind an olive tree so that she could laugh, and even David's mouth was not under complete control as he inquired tenderly after the Mayor's health.

'You saved me,' said the Mayor, crossing himself several times with great rapidity. 'You brave children, you saved me.'

'Oh, it was nothing,' said David unconcernedly. 'We just happened to be passing and we heard you shouting. We were going just down for a-for-er-for an early morning swim.'

'It was in the mercy of God that you were passing,' said the Mayor, removing a piece of water-weed from his moustache. 'Undoubtedly the mercy of God.'

'What were you doing up so early?' said David accusingly.

'I had to go down to the fields to see about my corn. It just shows one should not do foolish things. Somebody should have repaired that bridge a long time ago. I kept telling them about it,' he panted, completely untruthfully. 'So now they will have to do something about it.'

It was fortunate that the Mayor's donkey had scrambled ashore on the same bank as the Mayor and was standing grazing placidly under the trees. Amanda and David hoisted the mud-covered and dripping Mayor Oizus on to the back of his donkey and accompanied him up to the village.

'We know two things now,' said Amanda in English, so that the Mayor would not understand. 'One is that donkeys swim and the other thing is that mayors don't.' She was convulsed once more with giggles.

'Shut up, you fool,' hissed David. 'He'll think there's something funny if you go on like that.'

By the time they got back to the village everybody was astir and their mouths dropped open with astonishment at the sight of their leading citizen, caked from head to foot in mud and leaving a trail of water, riding into the main square. Immediately, magically, almost the entire village assembled. For one thing it gave them considerable pleasure to see the Mayor in this distraught condition, and for another thing, nothing exciting had happened in the village since old Papa Nikos, three years previously, had got drunk and fallen down a well, from which he was extracted with extreme difficulty.

The Mayor, making the most of the situation, climbed painfully off his donkey and staggered to the nearest chair in the café. He gasped, he fainted several times and had to be revived with ouzo, and was so incoherent at first that the villagers were quivering with a desire to know precisely what had happened. At last, with much gesturing and much crossing of himself, the Mayor told his story and although there must have been nearly two hundred people standing around, you could have heard a pin drop. The entire village, it seemed, was holding its breath, so that nobody should miss a word of this thrilling story. When the Mayor came to the rescue part, the villagers were delighted. Fancy! The children of their English people rescued the Mayor! The fact that, later on, when speculating on the incident, the general consensus of opinion was that it was rather a pity he had been rescued, was not thought of for this brief moment. Amanda and David were the heroes of the day. They were embraced and kissed and plied with glasses of wine and those hideous sticky preserves which were so dear to the hearts of the people of Kalanero. Amanda and David were of course, acutely embarrassed and felt very guilty, and indeed looked it, but this the villagers attributed to natural English modesty.

Eventually, having been embraced and kissed on both cheeks by the Mayor, who was beginning to smell a bit owing to the mud, they were released by the happy villagers and made their way to the villa, accompanied by shouts of 'Bravo!' and 'Brave things' and similar encouraging phrases.

To think and talk about

A 1. Which one of the children is the leader? Give some reasons for your answer.

2. Why do you think David is, at first, not keen to accept Amanda's idea? Is it just that he thought it a harebrained scheme or is there more to it?

3. What tells you that Yani and the mayor don't agree?

4. If they do manage to steal all the donkeys what might lead the villagers to suspect the children?

B 1. How do you think the children will manage to feed and look after the donkeys without anybody discovering where they are?

2. Why do you think the children like the island of Hesperides?

3. In what other ways could the children have discovered whether donkeys could swim or not?

4. What do you imagine life to be like in this village?

C 1. Imagine you are the mayor. What punishments would you plan for the children if you discovered they had sabotaged the bridge?

2. What would you add to the children's plan to make sure it succeeded?

3. Which of the children is never stuck for an answer? What does this tell you about that child's character?

4. Nobody seems to like the mayor. How would you describe him and how do you feel about him at the end of the story?

More books to read

1. *Huckleberry Finn* by Mark Twain
   The famous story told by Huckleberry Finn of how he ran away down the Mississippi with old Jim the Negro slave.

2. *Tales of St Austin's* by P. G. Wodehouse
   You should find these boarding school adventures really funny.

3. *Catweazle* by Richard Carpenter
   A not very good eleventh century magician arrives in the twentieth century! You should find the way he muddles through very amusing.

Spot the howler

We are having Aunt Enid for lunch tomorrow.

Can you say what is odd about this sentence?

John stood in the middle of the room wearing red trousers.

Searching for missing words

In the passage some words have been missed out.
Can you be sure which words have been missed out?
Sometimes there can only be one answer.
Sometimes there can be several answers for you to think and
talk about.
How many words can you find?

Removing his coat and shirt he plunged into the water (it was
wonderfully warm) and began to swim to the mouth of the
bay. It didn't seem to _____ much nearer. He wished he could
_____ a more powerful stroke than the _____ stroke, which
never seemed to get _____ anywhere. What miles it seemed
to the _____! 'Perhaps if I closed my _____ for thirty strokes,
then opened them _____ it might look nearer.' But when
_____ thirty lusty strokes he opened them _____ mouth was
farther away than ever. A _____ barely perceptible when you
were in _____ was gently shoving him towards the _____
shore of the bay. Already the _____ was shallower, the
fantastic coral bed _____ up to meet him. Reaching with his
_____ he could just touch a submerged _____ but so prickly
was it he _____ glad to let the current float _____ over it and
into the _____ of the north shore.

From *They Raced for Treasure* by Ian Serraillier

What's the truth?

Read carefully the following two accounts of the same game.

Reds Robbed

Reds started the game in good style and it was no surprise when they opened the scoring in seven minutes. Although Blues had lost a player through injury it would have made no difference to a beautifully worked move. Just when Reds looked as if they would score again Blues luckily managed to equalise. In the second half, the referee, who had been having a poor game, sent off Reds' best player for a very minor offence. The game did go to extra time but it was clear there was no way Reds would be allowed to win. He allowed play to continue after a Red player was clearly obstructed and from the pass Blues scored. To add insult to injury the referee disallowed a perfectly good Red score in the last minute.

Blues Crush Reds in Extra Time

The game started on time and within minutes it was clear that Reds should never have started the game as favourites. Blues looked dangerous at every touch and would surely have scored first were it not for the fact that their best player was injured. While Blues were re-arranging, Reds scored. Lesser teams might have thrown in the towel at this point but Blues came back to equalise deservedly. In the second half a Red player was rightly sent off for persistent fouling. Into extra time Blues' strength and overall ability began to tell and it was no surprise when the took the lead with a cleverly worked goal. From then on it was clearly going to be a deserved Blues win.

Talk about the two reports and try to decide how the writers have carefully chosen their words to favour first the Red and then the Blue team.

Pony and Trap

Two men,
Fat,
Sat
One in a cap,
One in a sweat-stained, trilby hat,
In a small round trap;
Reins dry, cracked and flat
Lay
Across one thick-thighed lap.
But a trap
With the smell of leather,
And pony.
How can you drop
On a main road
On the clip, clip, clop
Of a small black pony
With a trap
And two men,
Fat,
Unaware of traffic roar,
Doing a delicate, trap see-saw
On the wheels.
If two round
Fat men lean back
They lift a pony off the ground;
If they lurch forward to the breeze
They squeeze a pony to his knees.
A trap
On a road
Today,
Towed
By a black pony—
And two men
Laughing and nodding now and then,
Followed by a load
Of hay,
Coaches tearing the air away
Like calico,

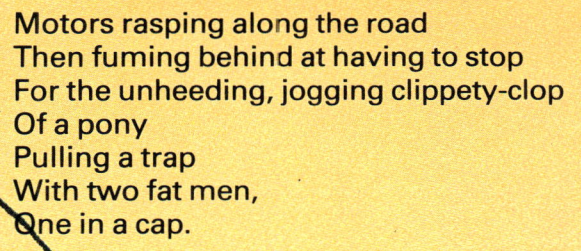

Motors rasping along the road
Then fuming behind at having to stop
For the unheeding, jogging clippety-clop
Of a pony
Pulling a trap
With two fat men,
One in a cap.

Gregory Harrison

How to use a book

You are planning a visit to a town or city.
The place must have the following:
   it must be of historical interest
   it must have interesting buildings to visit
   it must be near a river.
Skim the following passages about three places.
Would any of them be suitable for your visit?

Berlin

The great city of Berlin, like Germany itself, today is divided into two parts: East Berlin, controlled by the Russians, and West Berlin, linked with West Germany, and now surrounded by a high wall.

In the 13th century it was a small town, and it grew only gradually in size until the 18th century, when it became the capital of Prussia, a German state.

It developed rapidly in the 19th century with the growth of German trade and industry, and in 1871 it became the capital of the new German Empire. Many important industries such as chemical and electrical engineering grew up round the city. It had many fine streets and impressive buildings, but much of the city was destroyed during the Second World War. Since then, Berlin has been largely rebuilt.

Berne

Berne became the capital of Switzerland when the original 22 small states joined together about a hundred years ago. It is a beautifully laid-out city with some very fine medieval buildings, including the 15th-century Cathedral and the Town Hall.

The word 'Berne' means bears, and for many hundreds of years bears have been kept in a pit in the middle of the city.

Today, the city entertains tourists from all over the world, and is famous for making clocks and watches, and chocolate.

Cambridge

Cambridge is well known as one of the two great University towns of England. The oldest of its colleges (Peterhouse) was founded in the 13th century. During the succeeding centuries many other colleges were built with money provided by Kings, Queens, nobles and rich merchants.

The buildings themselves and the chapels often attached to them are very impressive, and their beautiful lawns and gardens usually attract the attention of visitors. The River Cam flows through the town, and many of the college gardens run right down to the river banks. These lawns and avenues are known as the 'Backs.'

Funny words

What word do you think the artist has illustrated in this picture?

Our language has a lot of words which are funny if you think about them.
Talk about how you might make a funny illustration of the word

clockwise

Draw the picture for **clockwise**.

To write about

Do you think you can write the story this picture suggests to you?

Upon my Golden Backbone

Upon my golden backbone
I float like any cork,
That hasn't yet been washed ashore
Or swallowed by a shark.

I never seem to want to snarl
In jungles all day long—
I've been so much upon my back
My legs aren't very strong.

It's all because a Pelican
I *didn't* eat one day,
Decided to look after me
That I behave this way.

And so, while Other Tigers slink
From tree . . . to tree . . . to tree,
I lie upon my back, and blink,
In Aqueous Ecstasy.

Mervyn Peake

Is it in the passage?

Anouska, Dominic and Marcus wanted to see a film. They found that the four cinemas within a reasonable distance of their home were showing films suitable only for adults.
Here is part of the letter they wrote to the managers.

Dear Sir,

You obviously don't think of the children in this city when you plan your films. Not one of you is showing a film suitable for children this week. This is not because there aren't plenty of films around. We know there are plenty so why won't at least one of you show one film per week? You should have a meeting once a month and make sure that between you, all interests are looked after. This will help you to increase your trade. Another good idea would be to have joint pamphlets printed showing what's on at all four cinemas. In this way people would not have to search all over different newspapers to discover what's showing. We hope you'll listen to us and cater for young people as well as adults.

Read the sentences below and then put them into groups:
   (a) Facts which are in the passage
   (b) Opinions which are in the passage
   (c) Facts or opinions which are *not* in the passage.

1. There are four cinemas in the town.
2. The cinema managers don't think of children's needs.
3. The children's films were all on the week before.
4. There are plenty of films suitable for children.
5. The cinema managers should meet often to plan their selection of films.
6. People waste hours walking round the cinemas to see what's on.
7. Children's films are the best films anyway.
8. On the week the children were thinking of, no cinema was showing a film suitable for children.
9. Cinemas should produce a pamphlet showing the programme in all four cinemas.

Read and remember

Can you read carefully and remember what you've read?
Here is a short story. Read it carefully and try to remember the
events as they are told in story.
Do you think you'll remember when you turn to page 142?

Traffic Jam

We had left home in plenty of time, just after six o'clock. My
sister Naomi was the fourth member of her school swimming
team. The race was due to start at 7 p.m. and the journey usually
took about 30 minutes.

What we didn't bargain for was a traffic jam at that time of the
evening. We came to a complete stop for fully five minutes and
then moved about a hundred yards in the next ten minutes. We
still had a fair way to go and Naomi was beginning to get
worried. Dad also began to show signs of annoyance and
stretched his head out of the window to see further ahead. I tried
to keep them both calm and offered explanations about the
delay. We all agreed that there must have been an accident but
as we came near to where several police cars were parked we
could not see any signs such as damaged cars.

Minutes later we saw the cause of the jam. A huge crack about
30 centimetres wide had appeared almost completely across the
road. All the traffic was having to edge carefully onto the
pavement to get past.

At last our turn came. We slipped past the crack and moved off
at good speed. Naomi arrived just in time to race and her team
won first place.

The company words keep

This is a painting called 'Children at Play', painted more than 400 years ago by Pieter Brueghel.
What is happening in the picture?
Make up your own title for the picture, and then write a detailed description of it.
Think carefully about the words you use, so that the description would give a blind person an idea of what the picture is like.

Reading for the main idea

Philip was working on a project about **Australian** history and came across this passage in a book.

In August 1860 sixteen men left Melbourne to cross the country. They had horses and camels for the journey and set up their base at Menindee on the Darling River. Half the party were guided to Cooper's Creek 400 miles to the north by William Wright who took a long time in coming back for the rest. Robert Burke, William Wills, Charles Gray, and John King decided not to wait but to strike out for the north, giving orders to William Brahe to wait three weeks at Cooper's Creek for the returning party.

Being tired and often short of water at Camp 119, Gray and King remained while Burke and Wills walked until they reached the Gulf of Carpentaria. On the return journey they had very heavy rain and had to kill most of their animals. Gray died of illness. Burke, King, and Wills struggled on to Cooper's Creek but their friends had unfortunately left a short time before. Burke and Wills finally died trying to march to Adelaide. King arrived back in Melbourne in September 1861, having been rescued by Aborigines.

Philip made notes of the main ideas of this passage. Here is part of the diagram he made. Can you add the other main ideas and use arrows to show supporting details?

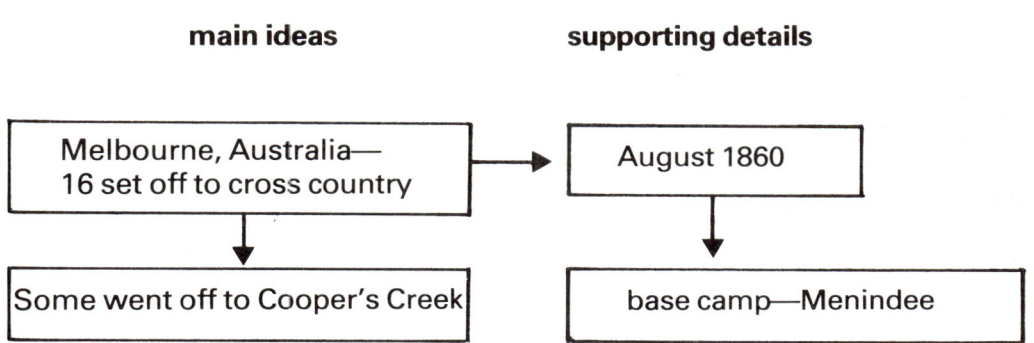

main ideas   supporting details

Melbourne, Australia—
16 set off to cross country → August 1860

Some went off to Cooper's Creek   base camp—Menindee

To talk and write about

1. Imagine you are the landlord of the inn or one of the villagers. Write a story describing the Mayor's efforts to catch the children when he discovers they sabotaged the bridge.

2. 'They watched as the donkey with great patience, considering the weight of the Mayor, plodded down the hillside and clip-clopped its way towards the bridge.' Add your own description of the Mayor to this passage.

3. Imagine you are either

       (a) the Mayor
or (b) one of the children
or (c) the donkey.

Can you write your account of the incident from one of those points of view?

Read and remember

Can you put the sentences below in the same order as in the story 'Traffic Jam' on page 139?
Don't look back to the story.

(a) Naomi arrived in time and her team won the race.
(b) The car was soon stuck in a traffic jam.
(c) The police were at the place where the traffic was held up.
(d) Everyone agreed there had been an accident but nobody could see any signs as they approached the traffic jam.
(e) The family left home to go to the baths where Naomi was to swim in a race.
(f) Naomi was becoming worried since they had quite a way to go.
(g) The cause of the delay was a crack in the road about 30 centimetres wide.

Act it out

Look closely at the story, 'Sabotage'.
Can you find a part which would make a play?
Write a play of the story and act it for your friends.

The way words are built

Do you remember how English has changed over the centuries?
Below are some words which have changed with time.
They are given in their Old English form, their Middle English
form, and their Modern English form.

Old English	Middle English	Modern English
sunne	**sunne**	**sun**
mona	**mone**	**moon**
steorra	**starre**	**star**
sweostor	**suster**	**sister**
steorfan	**sterve**	**starve**
(means die)	(means die)	

Talk about the way the words have changed.
The last word has changed in meaning.
In what way has it changed?
Why do you think it may have changed?

Here are some new words in our language.
Do you know what the words mean?

black hole	**bionics**	**chat show**
silicon chip	**greenfield site**	**digital watch**
safari park	**guerrilla**	**hatchback**

Why do you think these words came into being?

Acknowledgements

Prose

pp.	2–6	*The Snow Goose* by Paul Gallico, Hughes Massie Limited
pp.	24–30	*The Seas of Morning* © Geoffrey Trease, 1976 (Puffin Books, 1976), pp. 113–140, Penguin Books Ltd.
pp.	49–50	*Beowulf: Dragon Slayer* by Rosemary Sutcliff, The Bodley Head
pp.	70–77	*The Wind on the Moon* by Eric Linklater, A.D. Peters & Co. Ltd.
pp.	97–103	*The Ghost of Thomas Kempe* by Penelope Lively, William Heinemann Ltd.
pp.	119–127	*The Donkey Rustlers* by Gerald Durrell, Collins

Poetry

p.	8	'Something Told the Wild Geese' by Rachel Field, *Poems*, © 1934 Macmillan Pubishing Co. Inc., renewed 1962 by Arthur S. Pederson
p.	33	'The End of the Road' by Hilaire Belloc, *Sonnets and Verse*, A.D. Peters & Co. Ltd.
pp.	36–7	'The Tales of Three Landlubbers' © Ian Serrailier, 1950
p.	56	'The Bear' by Frederick Brown, *Every Man Will Shout* ed. Roger Mansfield and Isobel Armstrong, © 1964 Oxford University Press
pp.	60 & 80	'A Small Dragon' and 'You'd Better Believe Him' by Brian Patten, *Notes to the Hurrying Man*, Allen & Unwin
pp.	84–5	'I Had a Hippopotomas' by Patrick Barrington, Punch Publications Ltd.
pp.	108–9	'Posting Letters' by Gregory Harrison, *Posting Letters*, Oxford University Press, by permission of the author
p.	112	'The Man Who Wasn't There' by Brian Lee, *Late Home* (Kestrel Books 1976), pp. 7–9, Penguin Books Ltd.
pp.	132–3	'Pony and Trap' by Gregory Harrison, *The Night of the Wild Horses*, Oxford University Press, by permission of the author
p.	137	'Upon my Golden Backbone' by Mervyn Peake, *Rhymes Without Reason*, Methuen London

Pictures

p.	53	Winged dragon from the front of a shield in gilt-bronze with garnets from the Sutton Hoo ship burial, 7th century AD, The Trustees of the British Museum
pp.	62–3	Car overturned in crash, Fire at Flixborough, Oil on beach, from Keystone Press Agency; Boeing 747 over rooftops near Heathrow Airport, from Syndication International
p.	140	'Kinderspiele' by Pieter Brueghel, Kunsthistorisches Museum, Vienna